"WHERE ARE YOU FROM?"

D1641163

"WHERE ARE YOU FROM?"

HAVE YOU EVER been asked this question and did not know how to answer it?

This question, although seemingly simple, can make you feel lonely, disconnected, confused, and can often create an inner turmoil. Your answer to this question, where are you from, touches at the soul of who you are as it is woven into the perceptions of your identity.

As you turn the pages of this book you are offered a window into the thoughts and struggles of both a mother and daughter dealing with the common issues that arise from the question where are you from. You will lean into their experiences and connect them to yours. You will deep dive with the authors as they share their struggles and challenges faced as culturally blended people. And then, like the authors, you too will be able to find the insights and strategies to move forward to tell your story on your terms.

"WHERE ARE YOU FROM?"

A QUESTION THAT CHALLENGES IDENTITY IN A CULTURALLY BLENDED WORLD

ASHLEY TAYLOR AND LORRAINE TAYLOR

Copyright © Ashley Taylor and Lorraine Taylor 2022

All rights reserved. No part of this book may be reproduced, by any means, electronic, mechanical, photocopying, recording or otherwise, without the prior permission of the authors, except in the case of a brief quotation embodied in book reviews.

ISBN 978-0-473-63482-7

culturallyblendedpeople.com
Contact: hello@culturallyblendedpeople.com
Editor: Leanne Wickham of Red Pencil Ltd
Developmental Editor: Konstantina Sakellariou
Book Design: Rena Violet of Covers by Violet

This book is dedicated to

Wayne and Jennifer.

Together we created a 21st century family.

HOW THIS BOOK IS STRUCTURED

THIS BOOK IS structured in a way to be a journey of conversation and thought. It will inspire personal introspection and connection that will lead to greater understanding and awareness for you as the reader.

In 2017 Ashley and her mum, Lorraine, travelled to Prague to spend a week together. It was during this week that several conversations began that became the catalyst for sparking deeper discussions that continued for years. It became clear that certain themes were forming that all related to the challenging issues that a growing number of people face when asked the question *where are you from*.

Each chapter begins with a brief account of an experience that Ashley and Lorraine shared in Prague to allow the reader to travel with them to where each conversational theme began. Each conversation that was started was related in some way to answering the question *where are you from*.

Each chapter then springs into individual deep dives. Both Ashley and Lorraine individually unpack and unravel the main theme of each conversation they had during the week. As each share separately the viewpoints of a daughter and a mother, the reader benefits from the richness in perception from two different people, two different generations, and two different vantage points.

The deep dives are grouped into four themes that highlight a transformational journey. These themes are: Searching, Discovering, Assimilating, and Owning.

As the reader, you are encouraged to involve yourself in the topics and concepts covered by Ashley and Lorraine as they each share their story. You will be able to become completely involved in the last chapter when you, the reader, start your journey to narrate your own story. This book is the story of Ashley and her mum, but it ends with the story of you.

ABOUT THE AUTHORS

Ashley

ASHLEY TAYLOR IS an Air Traffic Controller in New Zealand. She was raised in Dubai and at the age of nine years old she moved to New Zealand where she currently resides. She is an American New Zealander by nationality through her mother as an American and her father as a New Zealander. Her life's journey unfolds through the pages ahead and is the basis of her inspiration for writing this book. It became a passion for Ashley and her mother to talk about issues and solutions to finding their identity as Culturally Blended People from two different perspectives. Ashley is keen to reach out to people in similar situations so that they too can feel confidence and closure in who they are as a culturally blended person.

Ashley and Lorraine are co-founders of the
Culturally Blended People Community.

culturallyblendedpeople.com

Lorraine

LORRAINE TAYLOR IS a Personal Branding Coach, Educator, Author, and International Speaker. She is an expert in guiding people to develop the skills and mindsets needed to authentically live purposefully, communicate effectively, and execute efficiently. She is currently the Managing and Visionary Director of the DO!brandYOU Membership Community and is the owner and founder of the BE!brandYOU Learning Community.

Lorraine combines 30 years of cultural experience in five different countries with continual research to understand the rich, diverse global audiences that personal brands communicate with today. As an international workshop presenter and speaker, she has inspired audiences in person in the United Arab Emirates, Oman, Bahrain, Russia, United States, Malaysia, and New Zealand. She is a regular guest on podcast interviews and offers her workshops globally online. Her first published book, *Be BrandYOU: a Personal Guide to Living the Life You Desire and Deserve*, has received reviews from people in 24 countries. Lorraine is a two-time Top Scholar at Massey University, New Zealand where she completed a Postgraduate Diploma in Business with Distinction and a Postgraduate Diploma in Education in Online Learning with Distinction.

Lorraine resides in the South Island of New Zealand yet continues to regularly interact and connect virtually with people from around the world. Connect with Lorraine at lorrainetaylor.com

Throughout the book, we refer to the term
Culturally Blended Person.

A Culturally Blended Person is defined as a person
who blends more than one culture into defining their
identity regardless of citizenship, ethnicity, heritage
or documentation.

TABLE OF CONTENTS

1

THE
PRAGUE STORY
BEGINS

TUESDAY MORNING
Leaving Dubai for Prague

Lorraine

"WHAT KIND OF clothes should I pack?" Ashley asked on the night before our planned trip to Prague.

We would need to have everything ready to go before we went to bed as we had an early flight to catch the next morning. Ashley had arrived in the summer heat in Dubai, a few days ago, from the cold wintery weather in New Zealand. She made a complete wardrobe seasonal change in one plane ride.

"Mum, what kind of clothes should I pack?" Ashley called out again from the other room.

"It is springtime in Prague at the moment. Days will be warm and the nights will be cool. Be ready for a good amount of walking," I advised.

After some time, we congregated in my room with all our things to begin the challenge of stuffing everything into the big purple suitcase. Being seasoned travellers, myself for almost thirty years and Ashley for twenty years, we still hadn't mastered the skill of how to pack light like Wayne, Ashley's dad.

I was looking forward to spending a week with Ashley exploring Prague together. This would be our first mother–daughter trip where it would be just the two of us. I always valued travelling experiences with my daughters. To me they were wonderful opportunities for real-life learning.

Early morning on the day of our departure to Prague when the city of Dubai was just beginning to wake up, Ashley and I were upstairs still doing some last-minute packing. Wayne hollered from downstairs for us to hurry up. Even though I am a Taylor now since marrying Wayne, I still run on Tanguay Time instead of the more efficient Taylor Time. Tanguay is my maiden name and Tanguay Time always marches to its own beat and is always fashionably late. A quality Ashley has inherited.

In no time we were settled into our seats on the Emirates Airbus 380 excited for the experiences ahead. With seatbelts fastened, the plane lifted off the ground and climbed into the atmosphere. Looking down on the sand-coloured buildings mixed with the many new high-rises that had popped up since our arrival in the desert in 1998 my thoughts travelled back to how my life's journey, that offered opportunities to live in different countries, had actually led me to living in Dubai.

My first job overseas was teaching mathematics in a high school in Papua New Guinea in 1987. This was shortly after I completed my bachelor's degree at the University of Colorado. The two-year commitment with the United States Peace Corps was meant to be an overseas experience of only two years. I had every intention of returning home to Colorado in the USA to begin teaching in a small mountain town where I would be able to ski in the winters and hike in the summers. Well-laid-out plans do not always eventuate. I did return to Colorado in the USA after my two years of teaching but only to plan a wedding to marry the New Zealand pilot I met in Papua New Guinea.

After our wedding, Wayne and I spent seven and a half years in the Seychelles, a group of islands in the Indian Ocean a thousand miles east of Kenya. Our time living there proved to be the most beautiful place for a long-extended honeymoon. I was thrilled to have the opportunity to teach in the International School on the island. I taught children from around the world and worked with a flavour of diversity of the other teachers. Wayne flew for Air Seychelles, firstly in the domestic operation and then as an international pilot. It was in 1998 when Wayne and I, with one young daughter in tow, Ashley, moved to Dubai. Wayne was offered an opportunity to fly for Emirates, an airline that was soon to have a global reach, in the United Arab Emirates. Our initial intention was to stay in Dubai for a few years and then return either to the USA or New Zealand. Again, well-laid plans do not always eventuate. Our initial few years in Dubai extended to more than 20.

Upon our arrival to Dubai in 1998, parenting was new to both Wayne and me. As those with children quickly find out, babies are not delivered with full instruction manuals. Within a year of being in Dubai we welcomed our second child. Once again, there was no instruction manual on how to raise children in a country where they were not citizens. Dubai did not have a system of naturalisation and did not allow immigration. My daughters were to grow up starkly different from the way that Wayne and I were raised. They were to grow up in a multicultural society outside of both their countries of citizenship. We were not intrinsically aware at the time of the impact of raising children in a place like Dubai.

The seatbelt sign went off with the sound of a ding and I resurfaced from my memories. Dubai had disappeared below the clouds as the Airbus 380 levelled out at cruising altitude. My thoughts moved to our upcoming destination of Prague only a few hours away.

After a movie and a meal, the captain's voice was heard, "Ladies and gentlemen, please fasten your seatbelts as we will soon be landing in Prague."

With years of practice up our sleeves we swiftly got off the plane, went through immigration, retrieved our big purple suitcase, and then happily headed out the front doors of the Václav Havel Airport Prague to start our travel experience. I was looking for the busses when Ashley said, "Mum, let's just get a taxi."

I considered it then decided, "No, let's have a travel experience and do things like the locals instead."

TUESDAY AFTERNOON
Arriving in Prague

Ashley

WHY DOES MY mum thrive on doing things the hard way? Why must we take a bus when a taxi would be far easier? Taking the bus would surely take longer to get to the hotel and be more labour-intensive. I guess that is the difference between a Boomer mother and a Generation Z child. I had gotten used to Mum's way of travelling over the years being more of a backpacker's style rather than a luxury tourist style. She was a teacher so her thing was to look for learning opportunities. It was her way of educating my sister and I to be more capable and self-reliant. It was still annoying though.

Looking around for an idea of where to start I sighed as everything was written in Czech.

"Mum it's all written in Czech so how are we supposed to know if we are taking the right route to get to the hotel?"

She replied, "This is what travellers do Ashley, they learn and become accustomed to the ways of the places they are visiting. It is about having street smarts and awareness of what is going on around you. Now let's figure out how to get to the hotel."

We went back inside and started at the information desk where the lady gave us some maps to navigate our journey. We squinted at the airport bus timetable that my mum was holding onto and then we cross-referenced it with the larger map of the entire city of Prague's public transport network that I was holding onto. We were like meerkats popping our heads up for a minute to observe what others were doing, then ducking our heads back down into our maps to connect our pathway from the airport to the hotel.

"Ah ha," Mum said. "Look, if we take this bus to this train station and take this train and then get off at that train station and get on to this train it will take us to this place, and we will only have a 15-minute walk to our hotel."

She was pointing at the foreign place names written in Czech rather than trying to pronounce the words.

"Fine," I conceded and grabbed the handle of the suitcase. We embarrassingly, to me, bumbled our way across the uneven pavement towards the airport bus station. I looked around at the crowd of people standing with us. I noticed faces of differing expressions with all kinds of fashion statements holding bags of varying sizes. I glanced at the digital sign near us that was being continually updated. I spotted our bus number and the Czech word that looked like the Czech word that Mum had pointed to on the map.

With 10 minutes to go I took a deep breath in of the crisp European air, then slowly breathed out the lingering airplane air. With my lungs refreshed I thought about how this holiday that I had been looking forward to for so long was finally happening. I had only arrived in Dubai a couple of days ago but I still had two weeks there once we returned from Prague. Since leaving high school in 2014 and beginning university in 2015 my trips to Dubai had become far less frequent as the responsibility of jobs did not allow for the kind of time off I had during school when I was a teenager. It was a weird reality for me to come to terms with not being able to go back to Dubai when I wanted.

I never thought that there would come a time when Dubai would not be as accessible as it once was. It was now 2017 and it had been over a year since my last holiday. Despite this little trip to Prague for something new to experience with my mum I was also really excited to get to spend two weeks in Dubai after our visit to Prague. I could not wait to spend time again in my hometown of Dubai after all this time. I could not wait to tan on the beach next to the Burj Al Arab watching the sunset, dine at all my favourite restaurants and enjoy the warm nights when the city was at its liveliest. I could not wait to enjoy that feeling of home that I feel whenever I am in Dubai. It was a dreamy moment thinking about all the things I was looking forward to after our trip in Prague when I was suddenly awoken with a nudge from Mum. Our wobbling chariot came hurtling around the corner with the next destination electronically flickering at the front of the bus.

The procession of boarding began. Arguably, there is nothing more embarrassing than stopping the natural flow of locals and tourists boarding a public bus. Our big suitcase with wobbly wheels was now proving to be a major flaw in our otherwise mediocre plan. All the other tourists had on sturdy backpacks, hiking shoes and athletic clothes. Mum and I had on our best clothes as we were abiding by the Emirates clothing standards for employees' families. The boots we were wearing were not made for walking.

Despite our efforts to hurl our big suitcase, carry-on bags, and ourselves onto the bus as elegantly as possible, we completely prohibited the natural merge-like-a-zip procession that was trying to occur. Once the other travellers realised that trying to poke and push around us was not going to get them on the bus any faster, they surrendered and allowed us time to heave and wobble our way onto the bus. Finally, we sat down and I held onto our bag in the alleyway with an iron clad grip as our chariot kicked up a low roar. It hurtled off along the curvy airport road with a sway and a jerk until it finally settled into a soft humming pace along the highway towards the city soon dropping us at the train station for the next part of our journey.

With the orchestral screeching of the train slowing down we arrived at our last planned train station. Heading out of the somewhat grotty underground station with only Czech signs directing us, we ascended on an escalator. Reaching the top, we found ourselves standing in a little city park bordered by classic European block buildings. We noticed owners and their dogs on slow leisurely walks on the walkways, birds fluttering on the ground hoping to find a worm or a fallen seed and overgrown flora covering the cobblestone paths.

After fifteen minutes of walking, we reached our boutique hotel in all her quaint glory. Underneath the windows were lush plants draping over their baskets and in the middle of the building there was a fancy red door. It had taken a total of 11 hours from the time we got up in Dubai to making our arrival at our adorable hotel room. Once settled I looked out of the bay window in our room on the third floor and noticed a small courtyard. In the centre there was a fountain of a young girl with birds on her shoulders bordered by buildings with moss covered burgundy roofs that had smoky chimneys perched on top. The scenery had a perfect European aesthetic which was delightfully out of the ordinary for me.

Minutes had passed and it was now 4.00 p.m. Czech time. We were ready to head out to find a place to eat dinner, this time dressed in our cosy spring jackets and boots that were made for walking. We opened the fancy red door, stepped onto the cobblestone path, and started on our dinner time stroll towards the Old Town in the chilly city of Prague.

PART ONE

SEARCHING
to go in quest of

2

A COMPLICATED
QUESTION

WEDNESDAY MORNING IN PRAGUE
Our First Breakfast

Lorraine

I AWOKE EARLY in the morning and was ready to start our first day in Prague. Ashley was still sound asleep. Slipping into my slippers I shuffled over to the big bay window and opened the curtains to see the glow of the sun touching the peaks of the surrounding buildings. I pushed the two windows open and the sounds of the city were heard as a backdrop to the tweeting and twittering of birds filling the morning sky. Such a beautiful day, I was ready to explore.

"Time to get up Ashley." She stirred and finally got out of bed. Soon we were headed out of the room to start the day.

Downstairs in the historically refurbished hotel building, breakfast was being served in the small room that bordered the cobblestone street. Ashley and I found a table for two next to the window and hungrily headed over to the breakfast buffet. The buffet was a typical European style spread offering a selection of cold meats, cheese, hard-boiled eggs and pastries. Both Ashley and I remarked that this was similar to what we experienced in Germany many moons ago.

It took me a little longer to prepare my breakfast but I soon joined Ashley back at the table and noticed her looking out of the window, seemingly deep in thought. I asked her what she was looking at and she explained that she was amazed at the different decorative windows on the building across the street. She pointed out how each storey had a different design around the windows which made each layer unique and original. She commented on how the layers each had a unique design yet they were all part of and connected intricately to the same building.

The thoughts in my mind were far from the windows looking back at us over the cobblestone street. I had a presentation scheduled for when we returned to Dubai. As a speaker and presenter, I often asked

Ashley's opinion. I respected her thoughts, especially of someone with a younger perspective on issues and ideas. Before we launched into exploring the wonders of ancient Prague after breakfast, I was hoping to get Ashley's thoughts and ideas on how to best present a few concepts that she could, I believe, certainly relate to.

Although Ashley looked more interested in the windows outside, I started waffling on about my speech. Periodically, I would check to see if she was still listening and was happy with her only two responses of "that sounds good" or "that makes sense". I continued to share with her my ideas and mentioned the acronym TCK when I referred to children that are labelled as being Third Culture Kids. This grabbed Ashley's attention the way that the cheesecake in the Cheesecake Factory does. She was now totally focused on what I was saying.

"Mum, what does Third Culture Kid mean? I've heard it before. In fact, just recently my friend I work with in New Zealand told me that I am a Third Culture Kid but I do not understand what it means."

I explained that a Third Culture Kid is a person who has been raised in a culture that is not their parents' culture and is not in a country where they hold citizenship during a significant part of their childhood developmental years.

Ashley thought for a moment and then shared, "When someone asks me *where are you from*, I want to tell them that I am from Dubai, New Zealand and America, as I feel that I am from each place in a different way. This never makes much sense to the person asking. Sometimes I find people actually disagree with my answer when I respond to the question *where are you from*."

I expressed that answering the question *where are you from* and having people not fully accept the answer is a common issue among Third Culture Kids. Ashley's gaze returned to the windows across the street, each with their own decorative designs. She then said, "Look at those windows across the street Mum. Each storey, each layer, has a markedly different design but they are all part of the same building. That is how I feel. I am like one building, but I have different parts of me, yet most people only see one storey." I again reassured Ashley that as a TCK it is normal to struggle with the question *where are you from*. I sensed, however, that just because this feeling was considered normal or common it was something that she was trying to understand more deeply.

With our plates half empty and our coffee cups refilled, Ashley asked me if I found that question difficult too. "You were born in the United States so I guess you would say that you are from there, but don't you feel that you are from and have a connection to the other countries that you lived in?"

This question about TCKs led our conversation directly into the complicated question of *where are you from* at breakfast on our first day in Prague and it opened Pandora's box. Little did Ashley and I know that our first breakfast chat would be a catalyst for a week of conversation sparked by experiences that we were to share. Our conversations would touch deep into our souls, thoughts, and memories. Throughout the week ahead we would wrestle with internal concepts of identity, defining home, and belonging. Each conversation circled around the seemingly simple, but in actual fact, complicated question of *where are you from*.

Ashley's Deep Dive of

A COMPLICATED QUESTION

IN FEBRUARY OF 2017, I was at work at a groovy bagel café in Wellington, New Zealand. My workmate and I were talking aimlessly as we prepared bagels on the line then hollered out the customer's name on the docket when their bagel was finished. During that morning working in the café, my workmate told me the story about her move to New Zealand from the Philippines when she was nine years old. I then told her the story of my move to New Zealand from Dubai when I was nine years old. We shared similar circumstances but experienced different realities. She grew up in the Philippines and is a Filipino, however, I grew up in the United Arab Emirates, but I am not an Emirati, even though Dubai is the place I call home. I told her how my mother is American, and my father is a New Zealander and that I was born a dual citizen yet was raised in a country that I do not have citizenship to. We were sharing our thoughts about home and memories when she said, "I know that there is a special word for people like you, it is called a Third Culture Kid."

I asked her, "What does that mean?"

My workmate explained that she did not know the exact definition but had just heard that word associated with people who were raised in a country outside of their citizenship. That phrase, Third Culture Kid, had floated through my mind before but on that day, it really stuck in my thoughts and I became confused about my apparent label. After work that evening I briefly looked into the meaning of the word Third Culture Kid on the internet. My investigation only uncovered long-winded articles that did little to untangle my confusion. I decided to brush it off as it seemed irrelevant.

When Mum mentioned the phrase, TCK, in Prague I told her that a friend of mine had just said that I was a TCK. I was curious to understand what this apparent label meant. In Prague, at breakfast, Mum explained that for me, my first culture is the nationality that has been passed down from my parents. In my case this is two nationalities being an American and a New Zealander. The second culture is the country and culture that I was raised in during my developmental years. In my case this is Dubai in the United Arab Emirates. The third culture is an amalgamation of these nationalities and their cultures. The third culture refers to a group of people, a culture of understanding, of people who identify with not being from one singular place but an amalgamation of places that they connect to.

After Mum explained this to me, I thought that the irony about being a Third Culture Kid is that most people do not know that they are a TCK. I mean it took me 20 years to realise it and have it properly explained to me. I began to wonder if any of the children I grew up with in Dubai knew that they were, in fact, TCKs too. I also wondered if TCKs were common in the world or if it is just a niche group of people.

At breakfast on our first morning in Prague I asked Mum if she ever felt that this concept of TCK applied to her too. I wondered if she felt a connection and identity to more than just the place that she was born. Although the exact definition of a TCK does not fit with my mum's situation since she did not grow up in a country outside of her citizenship in her developmental years, there are still similarities. She started her life as an American growing up in a small town in Colorado, USA. She then went on to live in culturally diverse countries including Papua New Guinea, the Seychelles, the United Arab Emirates, and New Zealand, each for a significant period of time. On top of that, she has legally immigrated to New Zealand and is now a New Zealand citizen. It brought me to wondering why this third culture concept did not apply to anyone at any age who has lived in countries and cultures outside of their original citizenship. From my perspective the places my mum calls home and the connections she has to the different places she has lived in are all blended into who she is and her cultural identity. I told Mum that there should be a word to describe people like herself and anyone at any age that can relate to being connected to more than one place and culture.

Throughout our ongoing conversations during our week in Prague and afterwards we came up with a term that fit both of us. The word that both of us felt described people like us is the term Culturally Blended Person. We both resonated with the idea of being culturally blended as this highlights that a person can be a blend of cultures that cannot be separated into pieces yet still is made up of more than one part. Our concept of a Culturally Blended Person is defined as a person who finds their identity as a blend of cultures that goes beyond one's legal citizenship, ethnicity, heritage or documentation.

In our conversations together, Mum and I have each tried to answer the question *where are you from*. It is an unknowingly complicated question for TCKs and Culturally Blended People alike. The conversations we had led me to ponder more angles of this concept. I thought about the times my mum had mentioned, especially during her immigration into New Zealand that led to her officially becoming a New Zealand citizen, that she had found that although she has citizenship to New Zealand and is currently living there, that she is not considered to be from there. I thought about the times that Mum had mentioned she does not feel that she is from Dubai even though we have had our family home there for over 20 years and it is where I consider that I am from. I thought about the times Mum had mentioned that the United States is part of her past and that it is part of who she is, but it does not fully describe her anymore. Yes, that is where she was born but to her the concept of from is more than just a place of birth, it is the soil that we grow our roots in. The reality is that there is not just one place alone that my mum can truly say that she is from and that she feels is a true reflection of her entire identity. I thought more about this question *where are you from* and concluded that the concept of where you are from is more than just where you are born or where you have citizenship. The question *where are you from* is a complicated question to answer.

I continued to reflect on the same concepts but this time in relation to myself. I thought about how I feel that I am from Dubai because that is the place I grew up. It is the first place I remember about the world. However, when I tell people that I am from Dubai they reply, "No you are not, where are you really from?" My perception of where I am from and where I have come from has always been centred around Dubai as the origin of my being, yet people do not perceive it that way as I do not look like someone stereotypically from Dubai. I thought about how when I meet people in New Zealand, they assume I am either Canadian or American but never initially assume I am a New Zealander because of my accent, despite the fact I have been living in New Zealand since 2006 and I am a citizen of New Zealand. I thought about how I believe Dubai is where I am from and is my home on this earth, yet I do not have citizenship or a residency visa anymore so legally I have no connection or belonging there. It leads me to this empty feeling of where can I truly say that I am really from?

With these thoughts bubbling in my mind, I realised I did not know how to answer the question *where are you from*. Honestly, this complicated question has always been a struggle to try to answer for as long as I can remember. The most difficult part of this question is that when I answer it there is this unavoidable reality that occurs where people actually disagree with my answer. Imagine that. I give an answer to where I am from and the response I hear about my identity is "no you're not" followed by reasons such as "you don't sound like" and "you don't look like" a person from there. This question, this complicated question, *where are you from*, has boiled down to the reality that I do not know how to answer the question. In fact, I have realised that I do not want to answer this question. I do not like having my life and the person I believe I am questioned. This has resulted in what feels like a puzzle that is impossible to solve leaving parts of me in pieces because I do not know how to connect them to each other as it does not really make sense to me either. I feel that I am a blend yet other people find this to be an impossible idea. To some people Dubai, New Zealand and the United States do not fit together at all but to me they are the perfect blend because that is who I am. It was not until the creation of this book that I truly began to see myself as a cultural blend.

As I began to seek clarity, I dove into Google and YouTube again for answers, hoping to find something relevant that could explain this blended identity that I have, as well as give me advice as how to answer the question *where are you from*. I was hopeful I would find the answer, unlike the last time I had gone in search for my apparent label, a Third Culture Kid, which just left me more confused. This time proved to be different. In my search I discovered the thoughts of others, others that I could relate to. I watched video after video of people answering the question *where are you from* and noticed a commonality among people who identified with more than one place. Each person in each video I watched who were asked the question *where are you from* began their replies with "Umm…well" which I often do too. Each person in these videos described the exact feelings I was experiencing too. They expressed feelings of being culturally homeless, rootless, misunderstood, not belonging anywhere, not knowing how to define home and above all not knowing how to answer the question *where are you from*.

The biggest discovery that took me by surprise was how each person responded to the question, "Where is your ideal place to live?" The responses were all the same and identical to how I felt. Each person's answer resembled, "I would like to live in a place with many cultures, in a cosmopolitan city, where there are more people like me so that I can feel that I belong."

There is comfort in being around people like yourself who identify with having a culturally blended identity. When we are around people who are like us, we feel that we belong. It became apparent that people like me are experiencing the same circumstances yet with different realities as our lives are each unique as to the countries and cultures that we identify with. Our shared challenge is to try to explain to people where we are from when we often do not fully know ourselves.

With the question *where are you from* there is an assumed expectation that a person is only from one geographical location, culture, and nationality. My reality, the reality of those that shared their views in the videos I watched and anyone else in the same circumstance, all struggle to provide an answer that fits that very slim, boxed in, expectation. Today the ease and access to travel and job possibilities in other countries makes it easy for people to move. It is easier now for a higher percentage of people to migrate, assimilate and create a blend of cultures without even realising it. Even though I say that it is seemingly easier today since air travel accommodates a quicker mode of transport, people have been constantly shuffling and moving since the beginning of time. It may have taken them a few months on a boat or a trek on a horse, but this concept of blending cultures and nationalities is a distinctive part of human history.

One of the more prominent issues with a culturally blended life, then and now, is that there comes a point in the natural desire of a human to want to belong somewhere. When you live a culturally blended life, either by your own design or by how your life has played out, you will realise that answering the question *where are you from* with one geographical place is difficult, if not impossible, even though it seems like such a simple question. To start answering this question it is important to accept and understand your untraditional identity of being a Culturally Blended Person.

Lorraine's Deep Dive of
A COMPLICATED QUESTION

THE FIRST TIME I recalled Ashley wrestling with the idea of her multicultural identity was in 2004 when she was seven years old and we were living in Dubai. I had just arrived at Jumeriah Primary School in the afternoon to pick up Ashley and her younger sister. I opened the front doors to the school and was caught up in the hustle and bustle swarming in the hallways. Tables were being lined up, displays were being put up and the energy in the hallway was noticeable. In two days' time the school would erupt into a collaborative celebration for

International Day. This primary school had 35 different nationalities represented. International Day was full of rich sights, sounds, smells, and sensations woven into the stories told by children and their parents from around the world. I was so happy that my children had an opportunity to grow up among such a rich global and culturally diverse group of people at such a young age.

On the drive home from school, Ashley told me about the homework she had to do that night. "My teacher asked us to write an essay for International Day. The title is *Where are You From?*"

Her statement was followed by a thoughtful pause and then she continued.

"This question asking me where am I from, what does that mean?"

Her words echoed in my mind as I noticed the growing silence in the car. I did not respond right away, trying to find clarity. I asked myself, what is my daughter asking exactly? Does she not know where she is from?

I must admit, up until this point in my life of being a mum I was doing really well. I always found an answer to all the questions that my young daughters asked me. However, this question, I did not know how to answer. I decided to use my dad's old standby and told her we would talk about this after dinner.

Our conversation after dinner had us both recalling the same event that had occurred just two weeks prior at a birthday party. Claire, one of Ashley's friends, was turning seven years old. During Claire's birthday party another mother asked Claire this question.

"Claire, where are you from?"

Claire looked up and quickly and confidently replied, "Dubai."

Bellowing from the other side of the room was Claire's mother, "Claire, you are NOT from Dubai. YOU are from America."

Claire looked confused. Claire had been born in Dubai. She lived there with her brother and sister, mom and dad. Her school was there, her activities and memories all existed there. Once a year, she would go to the United States to visit grandparents for a week or two only to return home to Dubai.

Ashley and I spoke about this event and she questioned me. "Why did Claire's Mum say that she was not from Dubai?"

I explained to Ashley that there were people like myself that grew up in one town in the country that they hold citizenship to. For people like me, the question *where are you from* is easy to answer as it is often thought of as the place we are born and have citizenship to. I explained that for people like herself the question *where are you from* is more complicated. You are connected to more than one place. You certainly have grown roots here in Dubai as this is where you are growing up. As a citizen of New Zealand and the United States you also are from these two places.

Ashley asked again, "So, how am I supposed to write this essay that my teacher asked me to write if I am from lots of places? Do I just pick one?"

"Think of the question as not where are you from but what is your story. Does that make sense?"

"Aha," she said, "I can write the story of me." And off she went to write her essay.

My answer to Ashley on that day set the tone for how she would find her identity. This to her would be her normal. It would be what she perceived to be a normal upbringing, yet it would be far different from mine. It would also prove to be quite different from the people that would be part of her life in the future, a few years down the road, when we set up a second home in New Zealand.

I recall that on that day when Ashley was seven years old and questioned where she was from that this was the beginning of a yearning inside of me to ensure that my daughters found a way to be able to answer, on their own terms, where they were from and where they called home at any given time. I did not know the journey through life that my daughters would take as they became adults, yet on that day I sensed that personal identity, belonging, and finding a place to call home would feature as prominent themes. I knew I was in for a great learning journey as a mother of daughters, both New Zealand and American citizens, being raised in Dubai among a bouquet of diversity.

I realised then that my daughters were going to have their own set of lenses that they would look through to view and understand their world. These would be different lenses than I looked through to view the world as I understood it. It would be important, as their mother, to make sure that I not only looked at the world through my lens but that I looked at the experiences my daughters would have through their lens. Home would be defined differently for them. Little did I know then, when Ashley was seven years old, that the depth of understanding would not be unravelled and understood deeply for years to come.

A few months after the moment when Ashley asked me that complicated question where am I from I was attending an American Women's Association brunch. These gatherings were held each month at a different hotel in Dubai. The speaker for that month spoke about TCKs (Third Culture Kids). It was the first time that I had heard the word. I learned then that the term Third Culture Kid dates to the 1950s. John and Ruth Hill Useem from Michigan State University coined this phrase to describe a person who has spent a significant part of their developmental years outside their parents' culture. It details that a TCK builds relationships to all of the cultures that they are connected to through living in a country or through citizenship, yet they do not have full ownership in any.

After my initial awareness and understanding about TCKs, I wanted to ensure that my children felt roots in one of the countries that they have citizenship. As you proceed through the pages ahead you will uncover that we made a move to New Zealand when Ashley was still young. Ashley's question when she was seven years old about how to answer *where are you from* unsettled me. It encouraged me to seek a way to settle my children somewhere that would allow them to connect to one of the countries that they have citizenship to so that they did not get confused by this question and could answer it easily. As you continue to uncover our story in the pages ahead, it is important to note that this was the main reason that we chose to set up a second home in New Zealand. Despite our best intentions it did not prepare me for the issues that we would face once we moved to New Zealand, many of these issues were not uncovered until after our trip to Prague. It was through the four years of conversations that it took to create this book that Ashley and I were able to delve into the deeper issues involved in answering the question *where are you from*. Our conversations shed a depth of awareness and understanding of how closely integrated our personal identity and sense of belonging is to the difficult, although seemingly simple, question *where are you from*.

In the conversations that Ashley and I had since our trip to Prague we recognised that the term TCK is limited to a set group of people. We discussed how it does not include the growing number of people in the world, for a variety of reasons, that perceive their identity as connected to more than one culture. It is important to us to find a better and more inclusive term that can describe people like Ashley and myself. We collectively agreed that the term Culturally Blended Person more fully and accurately describes people like us. A Culturally Blended Person, a CBP, is defined as a person who blends more than one culture into defining their identity regardless of citizenship, ethnicity, heritage, or documentation.

Today as I write this book in collaboration with Ashley and years after that moment occurred of her asking me the question *where are you from* followed by what that means to her at the age of seven, I have also taken the deep dive into understanding my own identity. My answer to Ashley on that day in 2004 assumed that I knew how to define where I was from and where home was to me. It was Monument, Colorado, USA. Little did I know then that I would evolve into a Culturally Blended Person and the question *where are you from* and where is home would become ambiguous. Little did I know in 2004 that years later people would ask me *where are you from* and my original reply of Colorado in the USA would simply not fully define me anymore. I did not fully perceive in 2004 that I too would struggle deeply and internally with identity, defining home, belonging, and answering the complicated question *where are you from*.

3

MISUNDERSTOOD
PERCEPTIONS

WEDNESDAY AFTERNOON IN PRAGUE
Old Town Walk

Ashley

"LET'S GO MUM," I said. Mum always had something to do last minute which always took longer than anticipated. Today I wanted to check out the Old Town properly as last night we only had time for dinner before having to give in to our jet lag. It was now the next morning after breakfast and I was rested and ready to leisurely walk on the cobblestone streets amid the old smoky buildings on the way to explore the city of Prague.

"Let's go Mum," I repeated a little louder this time.

Finally, we were headed out of the fancy red door and walking down the small narrow sidewalk. Our boutique hotel was nestled close to all the iconic monuments in Old Town. The intricate detail that was etched into each building was fascinating and not like anything I had seen before other than that time we visited Germany. The architectural styles in Prague were not found in the likes of New Zealand, the USA or the UAE, the countries that I was accustomed to. While we gazed, locals whizzed past and darted between us. They were clearly accustomed to these fascinating buildings. From their perspective everything was normal.

Ten minutes into our stroll we recognised that we were getting closer to the centre of Old Town. The different languages overheard started to increase due to the number of tourists in the area. We turned the corner into the large open street and saw again the statue of Saint Wenceslas in all its bronze, handsome glory. People were bustling all around as far as the eye could see. This part of the city was a well-known touristy spot with many international megastores that were nestled in the fusion of architectural styled buildings. I picked up a pamphlet from an information centre and read that the architectural styles included Romanesque, Gothic, Baroque, Rococo, Historicism and now the modern styles blending in.

Yummy smells were wafting out of the cafés and all the plentiful food stalls that we passed along our stroll. My eyes zoned in on one particular stall that had steam rising from the back. Inside the food stall were trdelník's (chimney pastries) cooking and twirling on a rotisserie. I nudged Mum and said, "Can I have some korunas (the local currency) please? I want one of those." Mum looked as I pointed to the trdelník food stall, handed me some money and said, "Okay, I'll be just over there," as she pointed to the stall that had long sausages hanging from the roof. After buying the local trdelník, I held the hot pastry in my hand watching the steam continue to form as it met the cold spring morning air before taking my first bite.

As I was eating my cinnamon covered trdelník while waiting for Mum, a couple came up to me and began speaking to me in Czech. This caught me off guard. I quickly wiped the cinnamon and sugar off my face.

"Sorry I only speak English."

"Ah I see, sorry," they said in accented English then wandered off towards the lady working in the trdelník stall.

Hmm, that's bizarre, I thought.

Mum appeared out of the crowd.

"That was so random. Some people just came up to me and started speaking to me in Czech," I told her.

Mum replied, "That's not surprising actually as your grandma, my mum, is of Polish decent. Look around at the locals. You do look like them as it is your genetic heritage."

I thought about this obvious misunderstanding that people had that I looked like a local from Prague.

Mum continued, "The Polish border is less than 150 kilometres, about 85 miles, from where we are standing."

I drifted into thought as we continued our stroll. I found it interesting how I had been confused with being Czech because of my physical features. It was an honest misunderstood perception based on my looks alone, yet it was incorrect.

MISUNDERSTOOD PERCEPTIONS

THE MISUNDERSTOOD PERCEPTION that occurred in Prague began a conversation with my mum that allowed us to dive deep into understanding how misunderstood perceptions occur when people are asked the question *where are you from*. Before I share personal examples with you to highlight the challenges related to misperceptions that the question *where are you from* creates, it is important to note that there are two types of misunderstood perceptions. The first one is the perception that other people have of you in relation to your nationality, identity, ethnicity, belonging and culture. The second one is the perception that you have of yourself in relation to how you view your own nationality, identity, ethnicity, belonging and culture. In this deep dive, I will be focusing on the first type of misunderstood perception, the perception that other people have of you. The second type of misunderstood perception, how you perceive yourself, will be discussed in the chapter "The Move".

It is also important to clarify that misunderstood perceptions that people can have about another person fall into two categories which include a misunderstood perception based on an Innocent Curiosity and a misunderstood perception based on a Deliberate Disagreement. Understanding the difference between these two instances is at the very crux of learning how to deal with situations when people have misunderstood perceptions about you.

Let us start by first defining what is meant by these two types of misperceptions. An Innocent Curiosity type of misunderstood perception occurs when a person does not perceive another person accurately but is willing to learn, discover, and become more aware of perceptions that are not like what they have been exposed to. On the other hand, a Deliberate Disagreement type of misunderstood perception is when a person is not willing to accept anything outside of what they know and what they have been exposed to.

When someone misperceives you without ill intention it means that they did not intend to cause offence. In this type of Innocent Curiosity instance, it is best to think of this situation as a learning opportunity. You, as a Culturally Blended Person, have valuable perspectives and experiences in the world that are worth being shared. You have deeper insights into more than one culture and can bridge understanding. I have had opportunities to share my experiences of living in Dubai from a resident perspective that has opened people's views to understanding more about everyday normal life in a part of the Middle East. Sharing wisdom of cultures from your own experiences is especially beneficial in a world of diversity and uniqueness. Conversations that transpire from a misunderstood perception that stem from an Innocent Curiosity are positive opportunities to share insights and to have conversations that will lead to more awareness and understanding.

When a Deliberate Disagreement type of misunderstood perception occurs it can often make you feel weird, different, defensive, not relatable and insecure about who you are. It is not an easy situation to deal with when someone questions and implies that your own perception of your identity is incorrect. This is my reality on numerous occasions, and it is a common experience of people who identify with being a blend of cultures. The fact that I have experienced multiple incidents of this and have found ways to manage these situations is one of the reasons why I wanted to write this book.

For me the conversation often starts like this, "Where are you from?" I often reply, "I am from Dubai." This is where my first memories are gathered from and they tie me to the place in my perception that I am from. The response that I often hear is, "No you're not. Where are you really from?" I find it so strange that another person completely discounts what I have said about my own identity and asks me again for a different answer. When someone asks me where I am from and they do not accept my answer it is clear that they have a misunderstood perception about me.

When people ask me *where are you from*, I really want to share with them all of me. I am not from one geographical place; I am a Culturally Blended Person. I want them to know that in my reality I am from Dubai as that is where I grew up. I am also from New Zealand, as that is the place that I have citizenship and have lived most of my life. I am also closely connected with being an American despite having never lived there as that is a big part of who I am through citizenship, close family connections and time spent there when I was younger. Many times, when I give my answer to the question *where are you from*, the questioner will often keep questioning me further until I give up and just say one place that I am from that fits their perception of me. When this happens my answer is being dictated by what the questioner perceives of me more than how I perceive myself. If you have dealt with situations like this it is important to remember that misunderstood perceptions can be very persuasive and can alter and warp your perception of your own identity. It is important to remember that if you give into these opinions and the pressure to change your answer, you will begin to falsely represent yourself. In trying to be accepted you will change or even lie about your answer to the question *where are you from*, subsequently hiding certain parts of who you are. Misunderstood perceptions that stem from a Deliberate Disagreement can easily make you feel as if you should diverge from your culturally blended self and just give the answer that is expected. Unfortunately, this will deny you the ability to support yourself in owning who you really are and will cover up the true reality that you, as a Culturally Blended Person, are someone incredibly unique and valuable.

To understand more of where the questioner is coming from, I have discovered that the perceptions that lead to misunderstanding often occur due to three characteristics; a person's culture, the way a person looks, and the accent that a person has. Below I share details and personal experiences related to each of these. I also signify whether the person asking is doing so from a perspective of having an Innocent Curiosity or if they are doing so as a Deliberate Disagreement. When we understand the reasons and the intentions of misunderstanding, we can better deal with them in each situation that we encounter

Misunderstood Perceptions Based on Culture

Culture is defined as the ideas, customs, commonalities, traditions, etiquettes, social norms and behaviours of a particular group of people. People of the same cultural group are united by common traits. It is important to note that generalised characteristics that are used to identify any cultural group are considered a stereotype.

A stereotype is a widely held and oversimplified image or idea based on a general understanding. A stereotype means that a person can have a preconceived perception, an awareness, and an expectation of the generalised idea of the characteristics of a culture and the individuals within. Stereotypes may be based on some truth but they are generalisations. Stereotypes can also be exaggerated and may not be an accurate representation of an individual or group.

Even though stereotypes are generalisations they are useful as they paint a picture of expectation. For example, when a person decides to travel to a foreign country that they are unfamiliar with they may want to have a preconceived idea of what to expect of the culture and social norms. Stereotypes offer a source of perception so that one can gain a degree of knowledge about something unfamiliar to them. It gives a person a sense of what the people are like, what the common social norms are, and how to be respectful to the culture of the country they are visiting. A person who has an Innocent Curiosity will travel to the country with an open mind to learn more about the people and not just see them from the viewpoint of the stereotype.

When someone asks you the question *where are you from* you may answer by stating a nationality, a region of the world, an area in a country, or anything you identify with for that matter. Each place that you specify will be associated with a culture. This culture will have a stereotype which may be perceived incorrectly by others. Some cultures have a positive stereotype while other cultures have a negative stereotype. How someone views a culture stereotypically, positively or negatively, is dependent on what that person has been exposed to and where they are getting their information from. I had to learn to identify the intent of the person asking me where I was from as that would help me to deal with answering the question. I had to realise that not all people will be curious or interested in knowing my full identity and would actually disagree with me. I had to learn to not be influenced negatively by the fact that a person did not want to change their misunderstood perceptions.

When someone asks questions that become Deliberate Disagreements, where a questioner persists in believing in a cultural stereotype and questions you in an offensive manner, two types of situations will arise. Firstly, a defensive conversation between you and the questioner will start which basically throws crocodiles in the moat around the castle of cultural understanding and open-mindedness. Secondly, as a Culturally Blended Person deeply connected to multiple cultures, it can make you feel insecure about who you are. It can make you feel as if you should change your answer to the question *where are you from* or hide your true identity. When these two situations occur, they are not positive. They deny you the right to fully own your culturally blended identity which reflects your true self. These situations can make you feel confused about who you truly are and will discourage you from conversing with people about the important cultural perspectives and insights you have and can share.

My issue with misunderstood perceptions relating to culture begins with my internal and personal identity that is connected to Dubai which is commonly associated with the broader region of the Middle East. I have many times said, "I am from Dubai" and I regularly get asked follow-up questions surrounding the stereotypes that people have of the Middle East and are voiced in a way as a series of deliberate disagreements.

A point I want to make to ensure clarity of understanding is that the Middle East is a subcontinent of Asia with multiple countries within. Although each country within the Middle East has aspects that are similar, it is important to note that each country is not exactly the same. This is similar to people assuming that Canadians and Americans are the same, or Americans and Mexicans are the same, or that Australians and New Zealanders are the same. These pairs of countries are similar in terms of location but they also hold distinctive characteristics. Although countries can share the same border or be part of the same continent or even be in the same region of the world, it cannot be assumed that the people and their respective cultures in these countries are the same.

Throughout my life people have expressed very negative stereotypical perceptions of Middle Eastern culture (which is a very broad generalisation of an entire subcontinent) when I mention my connection to Dubai. This occurs almost always from people who have never been to a Middle Eastern country yet still hold firmly onto strong stereotypical perceptions. They believe, without question, the information gathered from news, movies, television shows, social media channels, politics and dark humour. They gain knowledge from such sources that are riddled with stereotypical misunderstood perceptions and do not represent the people that I know in the Middle East. Unfortunately, people believe the stereotypes and disregard my experience. To them their perception is the truth and nothing but the truth. I am often asked how bad it is to live in the Middle East as a woman and if I must wear an abaya. I tell people that I am not treated badly as a woman and I do not have to wear an abaya since I am not Muslim. I go on to say that due to the conservative nature of Islam I choose to cover my shoulders and knees out of respect which usually brings on comments from the questioner that they cannot believe I have to go against my will, so to speak, and cover myself up. Again, I say that it is simply out of respect for the local norms and culture. Respect is a valuable act of peace. You may have experienced something similar to this in your own culturally blended situation.

I am often asked about Ramadan. I tell people that during Ramadan we do not eat in public unless it is in the walled eating areas for non-Muslims. People are often shocked and reply arguing that such restrictions are against one's free rights and that I should not have to concede to a religion that is not one that I follow. They do not listen to understand that within the context of the culture this is normal and acceptable for non-Muslims to participate out of respect and that the entire practice of Ramadan is meaningful and historic.

I am often asked if it is scary to live in the Middle East. I tell people that living in Dubai is no scarier than living in any other city in the world and that despite what the news platforms say I have never found it scary being a westernised person living in Dubai, one with an American passport that I frequently used when going through the border. Sometimes the response I receive from people is quite literally a gasp as if what I have said cannot be true. I have even been told by people who have never been in the Middle East that I must not have experienced the 'real' Middle East.

As I continued to experience these Deliberate Disagreements that were connected to how I perceived my personal identity, I continually felt misunderstood. I began to feel frustrated with people when they believed stereotypical views of a culture I was raised amongst and did not believe my point of view. I came to realise that because of repeated negative experiences of answering this question I was becoming more and more defensive, withdrawn and was often left with this horrible empty feeling inside. If you have had similar feelings, it is important to know this is a normal human reaction. If we repeatedly have a negative experience, we naturally build up walls to protect ourselves. As a Culturally Blended Person, I needed to become more mindful of misunderstood perceptions and the reason behind why they are made. I began to learn how to navigate a conversation in a way that facilitated a learning opportunity or alternatively how to end the conversation before a negatively fuelled debate ensued. It is in this way that I was able to avoid the situations that attacked my personal view of my own identity and the cultures that are important to me. If you have had similar experiences always remember that your identity is yours and it is unique to you.

Another stereotype that I have experienced is based on the fact that I am also an American. I have dual citizenship. I am an American citizen and a New Zealand citizen. I have experienced misunderstood perceptions with being an American. Firstly, I want to share that everyone has personal likes and dislikes which is absolutely acceptable, yet it is when those personal dislikes lead into how one treats an individual or group from a stereotypical perspective that is the problem. Regarding news, movies, television shows, politics, and dark humour the stereotype of an American is often viewed as people who are loud, rude, and obnoxious. There have been countless times in my life when I have overheard people, friends even, say in public, "I hate Americans". I have experienced situations where a person who is seen as being rude is assumed to be American even though there is no way of accurately determining that person's nationality from accent or looks alone. Americans and Canadians can sound similar as well as people that were taught English from an American can say words the way an American would. This goes to show that at first glance, nothing can be determined about a person. Not every American is the same, yet they are lumped together in the same stereotype which is a broad generalisation. This is a similar situation that occurs for other nationalities too.

I have experienced feeling awkward and alienated when sitting among people who are saying horrible things about Americans, especially when it is not coming from a personal experience but from an unsubstantiated and stereotypical place. Once, when I was introducing myself to a co-worker, he asked me, "If you are an American and a New Zealander then where do you say you are from?" I replied, "I usually just say that I am a New Zealander." He replied sarcastically, "You should say that you are an American and see how people react." Situations like this have me at a crossroads. If I say that I am American, are people going to stereotype me and treat me differently before they even get to know me? There have been several instances in my life when I have thought maybe I should not bring up the American part of me when asked the question *where are you from* so that I can sidestep prejudice, criticism, sarcasm and negative treatment. If you have been in a situation like this, you may relate as it can make you feel self-conscious about who you are and you will begin to disregard the value in your own personal identity.

It is important to remember that cultural stereotypes are broad general references to a group of people and they are going to occur. It is important that CBPs recognise the value in the blend that makes up their identity. When someone assumes incorrectly or challenges your own perception of who you are this does not mean that you need to become defensive, hide parts of who you are and lose your sense of self. You can attempt to explain to those questioning you but if this does not create a positive outcome it is important to not let their inability to change their mindset be an attack on you. I have had to learn to leave these types of conversations and stay firm in the value of who I am and my own identity that is true to me.

As a CBP, a Culturally Blended Person, it is important to not let the opinions of people that deliberately disagree with your answer to the question *where are you from* affect your opinion of who you are. By reframing your mindset, you will approach answering this question in a way that will compartmentalise other people's opinions so that what they say does not affect your identity in the way that it might have done previously. When I was able to set aside my frustration with the question *where are you from* and develop more confidence in the perception of myself, I was able to approach conversations that arose more positively. If I was met with a person who just wanted to deliberately disagree with me, I was able to end the conversation and maintain a positive mindset of who I am. As a result of being open to the possibility of a positive conversation I found that when people did show an Innocent Curiosity about my identity as a cultural blend, I was able to share insights into a particular culture from my personal experience.

In May 2018, I was in Astoria, Oregon, USA. My uncle, aunty, cousins and I were at a historical site learning about an early American settlement while walking alongside the river. My uncle asked me what the locals of Dubai, the Emiratis, thought about me as an American living in Dubai. I completely understood the reason and perception behind this question of curiosity as it is a question I have often been asked by others. In this circumstance it was Innocent Curiosity. I was someone who had actually lived there so I gathered that my uncle wanted to hear my perception, so I explained. My uncle was receptive and open-minded to my real-life perspective. I was thankful that my uncle listened and that he did not try to argue his own perceptions based off stereotypes gathered from other sources. This is just one example, but I have had other experiences when people have been open-minded when in conversation about culture and their associated stereotypes. Misunderstood perceptions are bound to happen, but they do not have to continue to be misunderstood perceptions. When we as Culturally Blended People use conversations to educate others using our personal, real-life perspectives about the cultures we are connected to as a person, we teach a new way of thinking. We transform misunderstood perceptions into understanding and that is an important mindset to cultivate as a CBP.

Misunderstood Perceptions Based on Accents

Accents and pronunciations can be picked up from all corners of the world and they are not permanent. Accents can easily change and modify as people spend time with different groups of people or when people move to a new place. The most important aspect of this is that accents do not accurately, correctly, and reliably define a person. Despite this fact, the strength of an accent is what people generally trust in, in terms of where they think you are from.

It is understandable that people make mistakes about a person's identity and where they are from based off accents. This can be an Innocent Curiosity as people want to associate you with a place and use the knowledge they have to make an assumption that your accent is directly related to where you are from. As I have mentioned previously, making a mistake or having a misunderstood perception is not the issue when the person proceeds to be interested in knowing your definition of self and where you are from. The issue is when a person corrects you about your accent because they do not believe you are who you say you are because of the way you sound. This is an example of a Deliberate Disagreement. Often when this happens you will continually be questioned until you say the thing that fits the questioner's perception of you. These conversations can leave you feeling weird, different and not relatable. It can backtrack you to square one when you ask yourself this reoccurring question that we as Culturally Blended People are all too familiar with, "Okay then, where am I really from?"

I was born to parents who have two different accents, I went to an international school in Dubai with countless accents and I have lived in three different countries, only one of which I have citizenship to, so my accent is a mixture of several accents. Most of the time people assume I am American, Canadian, Australian or South African. Other times people look at me and frown as they cannot figure out where my accent is from. The bizarre thing for me is that people rarely guess from my accent that I am a New Zealander despite the fact that I have lived in New Zealand since 2006. Like I said, misunderstood perceptions and mistakes are bound to happen so when people assume I am a nationality I am not or only half of, I have learned to try to not let it bother me. However, I must admit that it is always the follow-up questions and comments that send me down the pathway again of questioning where I am really from and whether I truly deserve to call myself a local of the places that are part of my identity. As a CBP this can be a very defeating moment in your life when you feel that you are not a true local or that you do not fit in like everyone else. It can lead you down the road that you are not really from anywhere because when people question you because they do not understand you then you begin to question yourself. It is because of these experiences that are continually repeated that answering the question *where are you from* is difficult.

In May 2018 I was in Seattle, USA. My friends and I stopped into a Starbucks to get a coffee. When it was my time to order I said, "Can I have a latte please?" The two people on the other side of the counter and a lady next to me literally flinched. I said it funny from their perspective as I clearly sounded foreign and not from around there. This really surprised me as I am regularly considered an American by New Zealanders due to my accent. I always thought Americans would think I am one of them too, yet this was not the case due to my accent. Situations like these, solely based on an accent, may seem insignificant but they are significantly defining moments in terms of your personal identity which strikes at the core of your self-worth. I have a deep connection to being an American based on my citizenship, family ties, and memories from my childhood. That day in Starbucks felt as though part of me, part of how I view my identity, was not acknowledged. I felt as if I could not claim that part of who I am and the citizenship that I hold. That day in Starbucks is a stark memory of how the perceptions of others can pierce into the innermost part of who I am and strike at my self-worth, my sense of belonging, and the perception of my own personal identity. The thing that makes this even more difficult to deal with and spirals you into feeling so alone is that when these moments occur, they go completely unnoticed by those around you. That moment in Starbucks when I ordered a coffee and got the response that I did created a divide in my perception of my own identity. Yet, prior to that moment I have always felt so connected to the American part of who I am and then to so unexpectedly feel that I was not one of them deeply unsettled the core of who I felt I was and where I felt that I belonged. For Culturally Blended People these situations come out of nowhere and yet become defining moments to one's identity and sense of belonging. Moments like these can appear to be insignificant yet to a CBP these moments can often be defining moments connected deeply to one's core sense of identity.

During my ten-month working holiday in Whistler, Canada between 2017 and 2018, I had the opportunity to meet new people on a regular basis. During my first week in Whistler, I was out for dinner with some girls I recently met. We were all enjoying lively banter when I noticed the Kiwi girl, a New Zealander, sitting across the table from me frowning. She asked me, "Where are you from?" Then quickly added, "What are you?" This surprised me as I had been living in New Zealand for the past eleven years at that point and thought I sounded like a Kiwi.

That moment in Starbucks and that conversation with the Kiwi girl lingered in my thoughts. I thought for the first time how strange it was that based purely on how I sounded, the accent that people heard when I spoke, seemed somehow more defining in other people's perception of me than my own perception of myself. I started to consider that perhaps I am not a real American and maybe I am not a real New Zealander like I think I am. I started to question whether I was a real local of the countries that I had citizenship to and carried the passports of when I travelled. I began to think that I did not truly deserve to belong there because other people did not recognise me at first glance as one of their own. These situations made me feel isolated and snowballed into making me feel that I had no real roots. I felt as though I was a tumbleweed in the desert that is blown around in the wind, never being able to rest. As a Culturally Blended Person this is where misunderstood perceptions, regardless of whether they stem from Innocent Curiosity or are a Deliberate Disagreement, are difficult to deal with as you doubt and question your identity and belonging. I began to believe what people were saying and reasoned that perhaps I am not from Dubai where I grew up, I am not from New Zealand and America where I have citizenship, I am not a full local of any place due to my accent which is a blend of the places I have lived and a result of my parents and teachers who influenced how I pronounced words and phrases. I came to the realisation that accents seem to be embedded in how other people define where you are from and mine is relatively ambiguous. When these thoughts began to flood my mind, I came to the emptiest conclusion in my life. I deduced that maybe I do not belong anywhere.

It was during my time in Whistler that I got the most reactions with my accent. It felt odd to have people not really understand me and be confused by my perception of my own identity. I was frequently either assumed to be a nationality that I am not, or I confused people because my accent was weird, according to them. The way I spoke to them was like no other accent they had heard. The reality is that my accent, like many accents of CBPs, is a cultural blend. Due to this reoccurring situation I started to think I was weird. When people would ask me where I was from in relation to my accent I began to start saying, "I am kind of weird, it's a mix of American and New Zealand accents". I thought people would understand me better if I just said my accent was weird and professed that I was not normal. I thought it would be a way to avoid those unwanted follow-up questions by prefacing my answer with what they were probably thinking already or what I assumed they were thinking. Perhaps this worked in the moment in a few different scenarios, but this was not a long-term solution as no one wants to be weird. This self-profession of not being normal and being weird led me to think that I truly do not really belong anywhere and that there is no value in the unique cultural blend of who I am as a whole person.

These next two situations that I will share made me wonder if I should just lie and say I am something I am not for the sake of avoiding a confusing and self-defeating conversation. This is the detrimental problem with misunderstood perceptions as you can start to feed into the misconceptions of your own identity. Not everyone will have experienced such situations, but I know that they are all too common. I know people that are like me in that they have considered fudging the truth of their own identity just to avoid the follow-up questions they do not appreciate and do not make them feel good.

During the last few months that I was in Canada I started to pick up the Canadian accent. One time I told a Canadian customer I was from New Zealand, and he said, "No you're not! You're not a Kiwi no way." Laughing, he turned to my friend working with me and said to her, "She thinks she's a New Zealander!" On another day I was checking IDs as I was serving alcohol at work. These two guys handed me their New Zealand driver's licence and I said, "Oh cool, you guys are from New Zealand." They looked at each other and then one of them replied,

"Yea, do you even know where New Zealand is?"

These situations among others made me lose confidence in where I belonged and in my own personal identity. It is difficult having people frown at you and outright disagree with your own truth of where you are from based on your accent alone. It is difficult trying to convince people who are oblivious to a culturally blended way of life and who cannot see outside of what they think is right. It was also at this point that surprisingly several customers that I was serving assumed that I was Canadian. It was at this point I remember thinking to myself, what if I just say that I am Canadian in situations when it is just a passing comment with a customer or a person I will never see again, I will avoid having to dive into a full-blown conversation about my life. This I considered a viable option because I was sick of the confused reactions and misunderstood perceptions that were happening repeatedly because it can leave you feeling awkward. This thought that I had led me down a path where I realised that I was now actually considering options where I was thinking I should just lie about myself. This can never be a solution as it will inevitably lead to further possible awkward conversations. For example, if someone asked me a follow-up question after I told them I am Canadian they could then ask, "Where in Canada are you from?" Then what would I say? I would be caught in my own spiral of a misunderstood identity that I started.

I never actually did tell people I was Canadian but the fact that it crossed my mind as an option was a breaking point for me. It made me realise that what people perceive about me is more powerful than how I perceive myself and I just could not shake it off. It was as if they were the driver and I was the passenger on my own identity destination when it should be the other way around.

When so many people have different perceptions of you, you go down many paths of trying to redefine yourself. You want to find that perfect answer to where you are from that does not have people questioning you. For me, I started to tell people my accent was weird and that my lifestyle was weird. If you are in the same boat, then you may have your own variations of how you have gone about redefining your answer to the question *where are you from*. Diverging from your true culturally blended self to satisfy the misunderstood perceptions of other people is never the healthy answer. It is important that you value the cultural blend that you are and learn ways to deal with these difficult conversations, reactions, and replies from others.

An accent is only one ray in the spectrum of who you are as a whole, and it is not a defining characteristic of where you are from. An accent does not accurately and correctly define a person. It is so common for one's accent to change over the course of their life as well as be a blend of multiple accents which may be different to the common accent of the passport(s) they hold and the places they have lived. Misunderstood perceptions are bound to happen and you cannot possibly educate the whole world to be more open-minded. Your internal strength of your cultural identity and belonging begins and stays sustainable when it is first achieved from within. Mindfulness is key when faced with misunderstood perceptions because it is important to be mindful of where the other person is coming from first so you can have a more birds eye view of the situation. Mindfulness helps in taking positive control over a conversation with someone when they ask you where you are from instead of feeling like the questioner is the conductor. A conductor who dwindles you down to say the one place that you are from that makes sense to them but may not necessarily be accurate to what you believe of your personal identity. You need to be fully convinced of your culturally blended identity and where you believe you are from so that you are not affected, to the point of changing yourself, by misunderstood perceptions regarding your accent.

Misunderstood Perceptions Based on Physical Looks

People can make the false assumption that they can determine where a person comes from based on characteristics such as physical features and skin colour. A misunderstood perception created that is based on the way a person looks is very personal. You cannot change the way that you look, naturally anyway. When someone places a stereotype on you because of the way that you look and couples that with a negative connotation it can feel defeating and hurtful. I have witnessed people continually questioning someone because they did not 'look' like they were from the country that they said they were from. When someone vocally assumes that you are from somewhere based solely on your physical features and this is not the place that you identify yourself, it is natural to have feelings of frustration and offence. This can lead to you feeling as if you do not deserve to be from the place you believe that you are from.

Often the perception someone will have to where you are from is based on their exposure and understanding of what the people of a country, ethnicity and culture stereotypically look like. People's initial perception of a person is what they see. It is understandable then that these mistakes are often made when a person looks at someone else and determines in their own mind where they are from based on the stereotypical idea. For example, my ancestors are from Europe (Scotland, France and Poland to be specific) and I have fair skin. On several occasions I have been confused with being Russian, South African, German and Czech solely based on my looks alone. I have had people come up to me speaking a different language assuming that I am from the country to which that language originates due to my looks. I have had people ask me if I can speak English due to the way they perceive me based on the way I look to them. This is just an example and to me it is not necessarily offensive however a judgement on how someone looks in terms of where they are from can be very personal and offensive. It is offensive to be associated with a place that is not based on your life and your cultural identity but rather on a stereotypical association of how the people of a country or culture are meant to look like. I cannot speak from experience and say that any reference to the way I look and where I claim to be from has been derogatory, but I know that that experience unfortunately exists for a very large population of people in our world. In this deep dive I endeavour to encourage confidence in CBP's to grow and maintain strength in their identity unaffected by other people's perception of them.

It is understandable that people will have misunderstood perceptions relating to where someone is from and which racial group they belong to based on physical features alone. It is not always meant to be or should be taken offensively. Associating someone to a group due to their looks is a natural instinct to associate items together that appear like each other. Humans do this so that they can have preconceived knowledge and understanding of the situation or person to create

44

pre-awareness. If a misunderstood perception due to the way someone looks is based on Innocent Curiosity, a person perceiving you is usually open-minded to your story of where you are from. If a misunderstood perception on looks is based on Deliberate Disagreement, a person perceiving you is usually unable to overcome their initial stereotype of you and therefore may not fully believe your story of where you are from because it does not make sense to them. Much like in the case with accents and culture, Deliberate Disagreements can be overpowering and can make you change what you say about yourself to fit the perception that other people have about you to avoid more questions.

One of the challenges that occurs for many Culturally Blended People is that they may not look like the place that they have citizenship or are living as a resident. When I first moved to New Zealand, other than my accent, I was always considered a Kiwi kid because of my physical features which are typical of a New Zealand European or Pakeha. The term Pakeha is a Māori word to characterise someone whose ancestors originated from Europe. Pakeha and Māori (the indigenous people of New Zealand) are the ethnicities that are typically thought of when one considers the stereotypical look of a New Zealander. There are, in fact, several other ethnicities in New Zealand that hold New Zealand citizenship yet do not have the stereotypical look of a New Zealander. Due to this I have seen many occasions when people in this group, including close friends, are recognised for their assumed race instead of being recognised as a New Zealander. I have also witnessed people being continually questioned about the answer they have given to *where are you from* since the person asking could not accept that the way someone looks is not directly connected to where that person identifies with being from.

When someone says they are a nationality or ethnicity but do not stereotypically look like that nationality or ethnicity they may find that people will continue to question them until they say what the questioner perceives them as. For example, I have a New Zealand friend who has only lived in New Zealand, is a citizen of New Zealand and owns New Zealand as part of her cultural blend. Because she has the physical features that are not the typical Māori features or New Zealand Pakeha features, people often do not believe she is a New Zealander. It is in situations like this that a CBP will feel as if they do not deserve to be the nationality they are, that they are not a true local and that they are not fully accepted in the community that they find their true identity. People in this situation can be pushed to say that they are from where their ancestors are from as this fits the stereotypical look about them and it satisfies the questioner who already has preconceived ideas based on the persons physical characteristics.

On the flip side of this, due to the way I look, whenever I say I am from Dubai, the country I grew up in that I call home, yet I do not have citizenship to, I am met with questions as I clearly do not look like someone stereotypically from the Middle East. I have been met with laughs at the absurdity of it and frowns at the unbelievability of it. I have heard the same old question, "No, where are you really from?" This goes to highlight the point that people often associate your looks with a nationality, ethnicity and culture. If you challenge their perception and say something that does not match their perception, they will find your response unbelievable as they cannot associate how you look with what you say due to their limited exposure of culturally blended lifestyles. In my case, not only do people outside of Dubai not think that I am from Dubai but in Dubai I am perceived as an expat by the locals so I am not necessarily treated as 'one of their own' which snowballs into feelings of rootlessness and not knowing if I can truly belong there either. It leads me right back to the conclusion which is that maybe I really just do not belong anywhere. I am sure that there are a handful of CBP's that have experienced something similar to this.

Our world is evolving in a rapidly culturally blended way and people attach themselves to their surroundings, upbringing, and environment regardless of what passports, ethnicities, and ancestors they have. It is challenging to change someone's perception when they have made up their mind about you based on the way you look. To overcome this, you need to recognise that misunderstood perceptions reflect what the questioner has been exposed to rather than view it as a personal attack or a sign that you should doubt your own identity.

You have the power over claiming your own identity and writing your own story in your terms. You hold the true perception of yourself as a Culturally Blended Person. You can be strong and unmoved by the misunderstood perceptions of others even when they have an over-powering nature of making you think you need to change yourself to fit in and to be accepted. You can decide and know that your perception of the world as a Culturally Blended Person is integral to encouraging a more perceptive and open-minded understanding among the people you have conversations with regarding where you are from. By understanding the reason that people make misunderstood perceptions based on what they have been exposed to will allow you to finally view their comments from a more mindful place. A place that does not divide your view of your own culturally blended identity but allows you to have a broader understanding of why people think what they think and why people say what they say. This allows you to be more prepared for follow up questions and Deliberate Disagreements so that you can maintain confidence in who you are, unmoved by the misunderstood perceptions of others but still with an ambition to share your unique perceptions of the world, whether people want to believe it or not. The views that other people have of you should be put into a box labelled 'what other people think of me' which is not nearly as important as the box labelled 'how I think of me'.

Lorraine's Deep Dive of

MISUNDERSTOOD PERCEPTIONS

I RECOGNISED DURING my conversation with Ashley that day in Prague that she was confused but also intrigued by the misunderstood perception that other people had of her. Yes, it is understandable why it happens, however, being misunderstood by others when it concerns one's own view of their identity is a deep issue. Experiences and memories like this blend seamlessly into our beliefs about ourselves and they form a central part of our self-identity. Since our trip to Prague where these conversations of our culturally blended identity first started between myself and my daughter, we have continued to try to pull apart and wrestle with how experiences of being misunderstood strike at the core of our identity and how we view ourselves. We have recognised that when these experiences are not resolved they continue to chip away at our self-confidence, self-worth and belief that we truly have a place that we belong.

In this deep dive I will share what I came to realise through the conversations that I had with Ashley. I will be open with you about how I became aware that even as Ashley's mum I was guilty of creating my own misunderstood perceptions of my own daughter during her growing up years. I will also uncover the misunderstood perceptions that have personally affected me. Finally, I will share with you some conversations that others have shared with me about the misunderstood perceptions that they have experienced as Culturally Blended People.

Misunderstood Perceptions of My Daughter

I never realised when Ashley was growing up that she felt misunderstood in the way that other people were perceiving her. In my mind, Ashley and her sister grew up in Dubai but to me we were temporary visitors to the UAE. We were able to live there for many years because of employment contracts that offered residential visas. It was understood that we would not become citizens of the UAE and so in my mind it was always a temporary period in our life as a family. I now realise that I was thinking one thing but doing something else. I thought of Dubai as our temporary home, but the fact is that I purposefully created a family home in Dubai as this was where we were living as a family. As a mother I did what mothers do and created a home for my children to grow up in, to create memories and to find their initial place to belong. I also made great efforts during our years in Dubai to ensure that Ashley and her sister not only embraced the local culture but also connected to their American and New Zealand heritage through the regular traditions we celebrated, the stories we shared and the repeated visits to the United States and New Zealand connecting them to the place and the people there. I admit, it never really occurred to me that Ashley would actually perceive Dubai to be her 'real' home and that this would be more significant than the citizenship papers she rightfully had to New Zealand and the United States. Looking back, I see the error in my thinking. Dubai was where she grew up, it was where her memories began, it was the place that she was deeply connected to through her experiences she had as a child and as she grew into her early twenties. Dubai was her first concept of home.

The first time that I really recall being aware that Dubai was not just a place that Ashley lived but that it was actually a place that she felt she was from was when Ashley was graduating from secondary school. Ashley attended boarding school in New Zealand as a teenager. Throughout her time at secondary school, she and her sister regularly returned to Dubai on their school holidays. As a family we had two homes, one in New Zealand and one in Dubai. This would change for Ashley when she was transitioning from secondary school to university. This transition meant that Ashley would no longer be making the regular trips back to Dubai as university life and work life would now take precedence.

During this period, I clearly remember one specific incident. We were driving in our SUV in Dubai and I noticed Ashley was upset. She could not express her feelings too well, at least for me to understand. She just said repeatedly, with tears in her eyes and overcome with sadness, that she did not know how to deal with not being able to return to Dubai like she always had. Ashley is, by nature, a self-confident and self-assured young lady. The tears that were streaming were real and, in a way, uncharacteristic. I knew, as mothers often know, that this was a sign of something deeply brewing inside of Ashley. As parents we seek to understand our children, but I will admit, in that moment, I was hearing what she was saying but I did not realise the depth of my misunderstanding.

My understanding was that as parents, Wayne and I, made the effort to set up a family home in New Zealand to allow our daughters to create roots and connections with a country that they had citizenship. As parents we perceived New Zealand as home while we continued to be guests in a country that we did not have citizenship but lived and worked. Dubai was a place that we had a home for more than 20 years, but we always knew that it was temporary. One day we would leave when the employment contract finished.

On the day when the tears flowed from Ashley, I merely listened and became aware that I had misunderstood perceptions of my own daughter's tightly held identity with Dubai. I made every effort to comfort her as any parent would do. It was not until after our week in Prague, two years later and the long conversations afterward on Skype and Zoom, that I began to realise that the family home that

Wayne and I ensured that our daughters had in New Zealand was just a building to Ashley and her sister Jennifer. It was where they went to on the weekends during school time. For Ashley, her home in New Zealand was perceived as the boarding house at school but her real home continued to be in Dubai throughout her entire time at secondary school. As I understand now, the perceptions I had of creating a feeling of home for my daughters in New Zealand was not their reality. I misunderstood how my children perceived their place called home. I came to understand through delving into research that a child during their developmental years, the years that my children lived full time in Dubai, formed their identity based on the place, events and people that they were around. Clearly the perception I had as a mother was one where I misunderstood my own children. I viewed them as American New Zealanders who lived in Dubai. Ashley, on the other hand, having had her developmental years in Dubai, was connected intrinsically to being from Dubai as an American New Zealander.

One of the ways that I now explain to people who ask me how Ashley and her sister view where they are from is that I make the comparison with the ingredients of a cake. The cake represents their view of their own identity, and the ingredients that are put into the cake are the cultures, each in the amounts chosen by the child, as representing the cultural blend of who they are as a person. I am not saying that the cake will taste good if they put in six eggs and one cup of flour, but I am using this metaphor as a symbolic way to gain a deeper understanding of a culturally blended identity. It is important to visualise that each child creates their own unique cake based on the amount and type of ingredients they use to create their culturally blended cake. Even though children in one family grow up together, they will naturally each determine the ingredients and how much of each ingredient goes into making their identity cake.

Today there are many children born into multicultural families where the parents come from different cultures. Some of these parents raise their children outside of both cultures for a period of their growing up years. It is important for parents to give their children the ingredients of each of the cultures that they belong to through citizenship and through the experiences they have. The way that this is done is through the sharing of stories and traditions. It includes interacting with people, like family and friends, from the respective cultures that they have connections to. These become memories of meaning that weave into a person's identity.

I have two daughters and they have each made their own cake of cultural identity with the same ingredients, yet their cakes are not identical even though they grew up together and in the same way. As parents we cannot make our children's cultural identity cake by choosing the amount from each culture that they are connected based on our own ideas. We need to allow each child to choose the amount of each ingredient that resonates with them. It is important to remember that what resonates with them is not conditioned to how long they spend in a country or the legal documentation that may or may not exist. I have a friend whose daughter grew up in Dubai and then as a teenager lived in England. When she turned 21, she told her Mum she was going home. She packed her bags, everything she owned, and moved to New Zealand for the first time. She is and has always been a New Zealand citizen, yet she never grew up in New Zealand. New Zealand is where she finds her identity. She has lived in New Zealand happily ever since even though her parents and sister continue to live in Dubai and England. It is important to note that when creating an identity cake, unlike a real cake, that the cake is continually baking as new experiences are added throughout life. I now fully recognise that my daughters each have their own view of their identity as a cultural blend. This view of where they are from is continually evolving with new experiences that they have. I now make a conscious effort to view others in the same way. I make a concerted effort to not approach people with a perception of who I think they are but with a curiosity to learn about who they are from their own perspective, not mine.

Misunderstood Perceptions I Experienced

This book is not just about Ashley and children like her that grow up as Culturally Blended People, but it is also about people like me. As you progress through the pages ahead you will discover my story, perhaps like yours, where you did not grow up in a foreign land among multiple cultures but in a place that for many years was where you considered you were from and where you called home. I grew up in a place that I called home because by citizenship it was my home, and it was where I was born. The people in the community that I was raised in were Americans just like myself. We shared the same culture, the same understanding and each had roots planted in the same soil. The children that I went to kindergarten with were the same ones that I graduated with twelve years later. I was fully at home in the place that I was born and this is where I always considered that I was from regarding my identity. This all changed in 1987 when I decided to go overseas to teach for two years. The plan was to return back to my roots, my homeland, my motherland. It was never in my grand plan to have the life that I have lived. It is a life that continues to evolve, my metamorphosis of my own identity. In the pages ahead my story is shared and highlights the beginnings of me misunderstanding my own identity. It leads to me uncovering and realising that I no longer identify with just one place. I am a cultural blend, a hybrid, a product of the twenty-first century globally connected world that we now live in. The roots of my identity are not just planted in the place that I grew up and had citizenship. My identity is now grown in soil that is a cultural blend of the places that I now connect to. When people ask me the question today *where are you from* it no longer makes sense to me to merely travel back many years to the place I was born and exclusively hold that to be a place that I am from. I am now a blend of other places. I am now a product of the culturally blended soil that my roots continue to grow in.

In this deep dive on misunderstood perceptions, I will share with you experiences that I have had that highlight how someone else's perception challenged my own perception of my identity. It emphasises that one's personal identity is something that is exactly that, it is personal to them. This first story I share with you is my first experience of having someone perceive me as someone that I am not, based on my citizenship. I didn't realise it at the time, but this was a significant event as it signalled the beginning of the struggles I have had personally with my own identity.

After completing my bachelor's degree at the University of Colorado in 1987, I signed up to work and live in Papua New Guinea for two years with the United States Peace Corps. In Papua New Guinea I was posted to a remote place, accessible only by small aircraft. I was one of two teachers who had come to work from another country and would be working at the local high school. The other teacher and I were given a house to share. Alison arrived from England in the United Kingdom. It was my first time to share a house with someone from another country. We enjoyed the evenings talking, sharing stories, and learning more about each other. Five months after we had worked and lived in the small remote area together, Alison said something to me that more than thirty years later still baffles me. She said, "You know you are the first American I ever met that I liked." I was stunned. She was not saying it to be mean, she was, in her way, expressing a compliment. She was sharing her perception that all Americans to her were not people that she liked but that she did like me. I was confused. It struck me as odd at the time that she grouped all Americans into a dislike category except for me. I was somehow an exception to the American culture in her eyes. Somehow, to her, I was not like all the people that I grew up among, I was different. This perception was clearly one of misunderstanding. I remember that it struck deep inside of me and went unresolved for years.

As our conversation continued, I wondered how many Americans she had met that led her to this conclusion. Curious, I asked, "How many Americans have you known?" I was sure that she must have come in contact with a large group of Americans and for some reason they left a bad impression on her. Her answer further stunned and perplexed me. "You are the first American I have ever met." This was my first memorable time that someone perceived me as something that was at distinct odds to the perception that I had of myself. The reality for me of Americans, the ones that I knew and grew up with, were that they are kind and considerate people. It never dawned on me that people would just lump me into some perceived perception based on something that was not grounded in some form of personal reality. At least it was not my reality.

This experience still remains a distinct memory for me. It was the first time that I really felt judged by a perception that did not match my view of myself or the group of people that I was attached to. As the years went on, I continued to live outside of the United States and I met many people with this same perception of Americans as what Alison had. When I asked the reason, there was never a personal reason, it was always a perception that they had from a stereotype. Most often it was based on something they heard or read. Furthermore, I always became that one American that was the outlier. I was the one American, their friend, that they decided they liked. This was not a nice feeling and it struck hard at the core of my identity.

For me personally, I now identify with being a New Zealander as well, yet I do not think I will ever fully be considered one. I am now a full New Zealand citizen, and it is my home. My family, children and husband are New Zealand citizens. I have embraced the country as my current home. I am no longer an American citizen. I often feel stuck in this no man's land with no real connection to anywhere from other people's view of who I am. I am not an American citizen anymore, so I am not viewed as an American from a legal standpoint, yet, in New Zealand people often refer to me as the American due to my lingering accent. Interestingly, this lingering American accent is not heard by most Americans, hence they do not associate me with being from America. I have lived outside of the United States longer than I have lived there. When I did live there it was when I was younger. Yes, I have memories and connections to my roots, where my life began, but this does not fully define me anymore. It is important to keep front of mind that I no longer consider myself from one place but I consider myself a cultural blend connected to more than one place.

Another experience that I had happened a few years ago. I was at a shopping mall in Denver, Colorado with my good friend, always a favourite activity when getting back together with my friend. Coincidentally, Denver was where I was born and this shopping mall that we were at was less than 10 miles from where I was born. At the checkout the lady asked me, "Where are you from?" Before I could answer my friend said, "She is from Dubai". I looked at my friend in disbelief. I did not utter another word after that and pondered how I was born 10 miles away and my friend was standing there telling her I was from Dubai. I did think, how can I be from Dubai? For me and within my perception, I was only living in Dubai it was not where I considered myself to be from. How could my friend, who I had been friends with since I was young, not even consider me to be from America anymore? That was the first memory of really feeling disconnected from my birth roots. My friend certainly did not mean to misrepresent me. In fact, she most likely does not remember this happening. However, it was the moment that I clearly remember this unsettling feeling when people would ask me the question *where are you from*. It was at this point that I began to realise that this question *where are you from* was becoming a very difficult question to answer.

It is important to realise that when we vocalise our perceptions about others without truly allowing the other person to be heard we create situations that can be remembered by others and it can cut at the core of their identity. My friend never meant anything bad by what she said, however, it was felt for years after as I began to question and struggle with my own identity as a Culturally Blended Person. The main reason that Ashley and I are writing this book as a conversation is to inspire you to keep this conversation going. It is important to openly share experiences with others to allow a greater understanding of how our identities are being shaped by the interconnected global world that we now live in. It is through open conversations where we allow others to be heard and understood that we take the 'mis' out of the word misunderstood and change the word to understood perceptions.

Conversations with Others

The conversations that I continued to have with Ashley sparked a curiosity in me to really understand others who were in similar situations. Perhaps you will resonate with the conversations and comments shared below of people that I have spent time getting to know to understand their view of how they answer the question *where are you from*.

A couple of years ago, my husband and I went to Whistler, Canada and enjoyed a month of skiing. I always enjoy getting to know other people who are also skiing in a place like Whistler where there is a collection of local Canadians, as well as people from other parts of the world. On that particular visit, I met a local lady from a town nearby in Canada. Her name was Julie. She shared with me a typical conversation that she experiences on a fairly regular basis when asked the question *where are you from.*

Stranger: Hello, where are you from?

Julie: I'm from Canada.

Stranger: (taken aback) Oh no, I meant where are you really from?

Julie: I am from Vancouver, Canada.

Stranger: But you are Asian.

This is, in fact an all-too-common conversation experienced by so many people who do not physically look like the perceived perception of the place that they say they are from.

Julie was, in fact, born in Vancouver, Canada. She is Canadian. She has never visited any country in Asia, yet Julie is not perceived to be Canadian. Furthermore, just a note on geography that fuels further misunderstanding is that Asia covers a large area of our world and there are many cultures within Asia. To firstly refute the identity of a person based on looks and then to attach an identity label as large as the geographical area of Asia is not being mindful of the diversity of people we have in this world. I agree, a person may not have an intention to incorrectly perceive someone. I admit, I am guilty myself of doing this without ill intent, however, it is important to realise that the incorrect perception that is voiced can feel like a personal attack on one's identity. This attack creates a deeper scar when a person disagrees with your own perception of yourself and then adds, "No you are not. Where are you really from?"

I met Sep during the years that I lived in Dubai. Sep was born in Scotland and her nationality is Persian/Iranian. Her citizenship includes Great Britain, Iran and the UAE. When she responds to questions about where she is from these are the responses she hears, "How can you be from Iran? Your accent is different to all Iranians we meet!", "Oh really! I wouldn't have guessed you are Iranian!" and "You do not look Iranian at all!" Sep goes onto explain, "I do not blame people for their misunderstood perceptions. People build their perspectives mainly based on what they know and what they see. Most perceptions are pushed out through local and national media. I do not fit the general stereotype that many people have created in their own minds about Iranians. It is indeed one of my missions to change that with every new person I meet in my life."

In my conversation with Sep, she brought up an important point about how we react to people's responses to questions that seem to challenge our identity. She gave her story as an example of how one's answer changes to the question *where are you from* based on where they are located at the time. She shared that she used to never reveal the full identity of who she is. As humans we have a natural and deep desire to feel that we belong and this can push us to even misperceive who we really are. On this note, Sep shares these words:

"When I was in the UK, I always answered the question *where are you from* as Scotland as I am Scottish. That is where I was born but not where I found all the blend of my identity. The reason I simply mentioned Scotland and left out the other parts of my cultural blend was because I did not want people to see me as a foreigner. I knew that if I tried to explain that I was also Iranian that the perceptions of me would be misunderstood due to people's perceptions of Iranians. Once I was able to get to know someone better, I would gradually let them know that I was also Iranian but only after a bond of trust was formed. It was then that I would share that I was Iranian and that I also had UK citizenship and was born in Scotland. I now recognise that I was not comfortable with my own identity. I had misunderstood perceptions about myself. I also admit I was a people-pleaser. I wanted to say what would get people to perceive me positively. I did not want to be challenged by their misunderstood perceptions. Saying that I was from Iran in the first instance, almost always backfired on me. I realise now that it was people's lack of knowledge that made me feel this way rather than my own lack of understanding of my true identity."

I had a similar conversation with Suzanne but also unique to her. Suzanne shared with me that she chooses to respond to the question *where are you from* with the exact location of where she is living at the present time. Suzanne lives in France and has been there for many years. She explained to me that she does not want to say that she is from Britain anymore as she has not lived there for more than 30 years, although she is still a British citizen. Suzanne has lived a longer time in France than she has lived in Britain. She explained that she does not have French citizenship and will never be considered French by the French. Suzanne shares the frustrations that she, and many people who are culturally blended relate to when having to answer the question *where are you from*. She said to me, "I hate this question. The people that I know in France often start with this question as they connect a strong regional importance to the answer. They place great importance on the place that one is born as that then gives an indication of a lot more detail about the person, all perceived and only some based in reality." Suzanne admits that sometimes when asked the question *where are you from* she launches into an intercultural lecture while other times she just answers with what a person wants to hear to stop the conversation. Suzanne's frustration is shared by me and countless other people around the world.

My friend Saira was born in India but grew up and has lived in Dubai most of her life. She has since moved to Bahrain. She is a citizen of India but is considered a non-resident Indian, an NRI, from birth. I asked her, "How do you respond to the question *where are you from* when asked?" She explained that despite the citizenship papers and status as a non-resident Indian, she feels that she is from Dubai. It is where she grew up and it is where she considers home. For her, Dubai holds the memories of her childhood. The sights, the smells, and the sounds of Dubai are part of the story of Saira's identity. I asked if she ever says that she is from India. She shared with me that she is not deeply connected to the country of her citizenship as a non-resident Indian. She feels mostly connected to her fellow NRIs especially the ones that have grown up in the Middle East. She mentioned that there is a feeling of 'we' as a common thread that characterises who we are as non-resident Indians. After pondering my conversation with Saira, I thought what it would feel like to have an identity tag like non-resident Indian that actually does not allow a person to put down firm roots. Saira does not have citizenship to the UAE so is unable to put down firm roots in Dubai, even though she will claim her identity to Dubai as that is where she grew up and lived for many years. Saira shares such a common conversation that I have had with so many which is this feeling of not truly belonging to any one geographical place. Saira is like many others, and similar to Ashley, in that the place that she considers that she is from is grown from a deep connection based on experiences and has little to do with legality and the perceptions of others.

Samir has a similar story, yet also different in its own uniqueness. I asked Samir, "How do you answer the question *where are you from?*" He shared that the answer that he often gives is one that will let people recognise the blend in his identity and admits that it is a far longer answer than anyone is expecting. The question *where are you from* is often used as an introductory, get to know you question that has the expectation that you will answer with one geographical place. Samir's answer is much longer and far more accurate. "I am an American and was born in Cincinnati, Ohio. I should mention that I lived in North Carolina for 20 years and this is where I consider home in the United States. When I was six, we moved to Kuwait. I lived there for eight years, then I moved to Egypt for two years, then to Mallorca, Spain for two years followed by 20 years in North Carolina, USA. I am now in my twelfth year of living in England, UK." Samir shares the challenges that he has dealt with regarding misunderstood perceptions. "In the UK, because of my appearance, people will assume that I am from India or Pakistan as that is what they assume my identity to be. However, when I begin speaking, my accent is clearly American. Interestingly, once the American accent is heard I notice being treated different-ly." Samir shares a specific example as to the challenges that exist as to how perceptions of who we are can change overtime. "After living in the UK for 10 years I was fully considered an American among the people in my local community. When I returned to North Carolina on a trip I felt as if I was going home but I got the distinct impression that I was being treated as an outsider who was now perceived with a distinct Egyptian appearance. It was an uncanny feeling to feel less American in America than I did outside of America."

Perception is a Lens

Perception acts as a lens through which we view ourselves and the world around us. Our perceptions influence how we interpret, understand, and view others. Perceptions are also often used as we view and define ourselves. The deep conversations that Ashley and I have had during and since our time in Prague have clearly made me aware of how our identity is intertwined closely with how others perceive us and how we perceive ourselves.

Today we live in a world of multiplicity in identity. A person's real identity is on the inside as opposed to the outside. The perceptions that others have, and the perceptions that we have, of a person are often based on outside characteristics such as skin colour, religion, accent, physical characteristics, mannerisms, and other external things that make a person.

I am not suggesting that we stop asking the question *where are you from* as it is a natural way to try to build a connection with someone when we meet them. I am suggesting that we make a great effort to not ask the question looking through our own lens of perception but to seek to look through the lens of the person we are talking to.

4

SEARCH
FOR
IDENTITY

WEDNESDAY EVENING IN PRAGUE
Visit To the Astronomical Clock

Lorraine

THE SUN WAS beginning to set against the backdrop of the historic city. Rounding the curvy narrow walkway, the cobblestones opened into the expansive, wide, and triumphant Old Town Square. The energy immediately increased with the surrounding bustle and noise of the people. Groups of friends sat howling and laughing while clinking their beers on stools outside bars. People and families were posing for photos in glamorous coats in front of the picturesque buildings. Huddles of admiring tourists were roaming around in all directions, walking in and out of the various entrances and exits to the Old Town Square. I stopped in my tracks momentarily gazing at this enchanting place.

In the distance the Astronomical Clock stood in all its grandeur as the magically engineered performance came to its close. There was a huddle of people with their phones held up high at the bottom of the building that the clock was built into. We were a bit far away and only caught the end of the moving figurines as they rotated back inside the clock that was situated in the top tower of the building. The little doors closed behind them only to reopen when the next hour struck.

Our tummies were hungry for dinner so we looked for a restaurant right up close to the clock to ensure that we could have a real dinner and a show when the next hour ticked around. We found the perfect spot at a big outside restaurant with a sloping red and white cabana. There were clusters of little square tables nestled together and bordered by a short fence with little baskets of flowers hanging from the top rail.

While we were waiting to be seated at our table, I picked up a pamphlet that shared details of the Astronomical Clock and learned it had been operating since the 1400s. It is the third oldest astronomical clock in the world and the only one still working. Amid everything the world has been through since the clock's creation in the 1400s, this clock has continuously ticked away. It had a medieval and gothic appeal to it much like the grey and smoky building it was built into.

On closer inspection I noticed the many dials within that displayed the so-called 'planetary state of the universe'. I could see the zodiac ring, the ancient and present-day time ring, the placement of the sun and moon all moving simultaneously and individually.

After being ushered to our table we were handed menus written all in Czech but thankfully with English translations underneath. I was reading the menu looking for a local dish to fit the moment when Ashley whispered, "I want one of those" and pointed at a big frothy beer on the table near us. I knew Prague was renowned for their beers and I was looking forward to trying one myself. In a flash, two frothy Czech beers were served and we took a sip soaking in the flavour and surrounding atmosphere. There was colourful diversity among the tourists and it was interesting to see people from all corners of the globe gathered together in one historical place all doing the same thing, simply enjoying being there and in the moment.

We were both sitting in silent wonder and amusement when Ashley asked, "Why did Grandma Tanguay's family move from Poland to the United States as you mentioned earlier?" I took a moment recalling memories and stories that my mom and grandma, Ashley's great grandma, had told me. "The Spychalla's, your grandma's maiden name, left Poland in the late 1800s. There was famine, starvation, war, and poverty defining the lives of many in the country at that time. They wanted what the new country America had to offer, a fresh start. One day they boarded a ship never to return. They created a new home in Wisconsin with only the things packed in their suitcases. They had to find and search for their new identity in a new land."

After a few more sips of beer I continued, "It would have been tough you know for all the people that chose to immigrate and leave their homes years ago. Travel was not like it is today as back then so many who left never returned. In the late 1800s, people in many parts of the world decided to leave their homes and immigrate to America because it was perceived as the land of economic opportunity and personal freedom." I checked my phone to find the exact details, "12 million immigrants arrived in America between 1870 and 1900."

Ashley pondered this for a moment, took another sip of beer and added, "There would have been a lot of tugging and pulling then as the new and old American's searched, clashed and collectively tried to define what the evolving definition, identity and meaning of an American was in those days. This is not different to what is happening right now. So many countries have new people arriving and bringing essences of their cultures and identity to the new country. Our Polish ancestors would have had to search for a new identity. One that would be part of their old life and their new life. I feel like that too."

These words lingered as the ensemble of public chatter filled the air once more. Our waiter joyfully arrived with two dishes and placed them in front of us. With gusto he said in Czech accented English, "Enjoy ladies!" After a couple of bites in we noticed the hourly huddle of tourists gathering underneath the Astronomical Clock and we eagerly waited for the show of figurines and revolving parts to entertain us as we finished our meal.

Ashley's Deep Dive of

SEARCH FOR IDENTITY

WHEN YOU ARE asked the question *where are you from* and you do not have a clear answer you enter into a state of searching for the right answer, searching for who you are, and searching for validity in your own identity. This search can often feel as if there is no end. As the search continues you begin to feel rootless, as if you do not belong anywhere. You feel that you are not part of any one place which leaves you feeling isolated and alone because you can feel different than the people around you. The thing to recognise is that your answer to the question what is my identity, and your answer to the question where am I from are related to each other. You might wonder which question should be answered first? It is like the chicken and the egg theory in determining which one comes first. Do you search for your identity as that determines the places that you are connected to and that you would say that you are from? Or, do you first find the answer to where you are from and then you get clarity on your identity? Searching for and understanding your identity comes first and then how you answer the question *where are you from* comes second. Your identity is the entirety of you. It is like the house of you. Your answer to the question *where are you from* is like a window to look inside, it is a part of your identity that becomes visible. You may have more than one window in your house as you may have more than one culture that you connect with. Your identity is greater than and more comprehensive than just where you are from. This is the reason that it is important to discover and understand your detailed culturally blended identity first as this will assist you in answering the question *where are you from.*

In December of 2017, I was in Whistler, Canada. It was a gorgeous sunny day and I was enjoying the opportunity to spend it with some girls I had recently met. They wanted to check out an op shop in the southern part of Whistler, so we hopped on a bus and travelled down the snowy road. Donated skis lined the fence around the snow-covered op shop and there was a short line of people dropping things off. I went into the shop for a little while but not long after, myself and one of the girls decided to wait outside. I actually had only met this girl that day so while we were standing outside, I asked her, "Where are you from?" She stared at the ground and started moving her boot sideways through the snow with a nervous tick. "Um, well it's... kind of…. hard to explain. Like I'm from Australia but I'm not like a real Australian. I'm a New Zealander by citizenship as my parents are both Kiwis so I am technically a New Zealander, but I have never lived there. I grew up in Australia and have lived there my whole life and I love it there. I don't want to live in New Zealand but I can't really call myself an Australian because I'm technically not. So, I don't really know. I feel like…I feel like I have no identity."

That feeling of being a fake citizen because of documents and technicality was a familiar feeling to me in that moment as I have always felt as if I am from Dubai but I do not have the legal documentation to back it up. The girl I spoke to wanted to say she was Australian because that is the country she identifies herself with as that is where she grew up. All her memories, influences, life and everything is connected to Australia. The difficulty that she experiences is that she does not feel as if she deserves to be from the place that she most identifies with. She feels weird saying that she is Australian when she is, in fact, a New Zealander by citizenship and that is the only passport she holds. Yet despite legalities, she identifies with being an Australian not a New Zealander. As I pondered this fact of life for people like me, I felt that one of the most difficult things to deal with is when a person finds their identity, either partially or wholly, in a place that they have no legal documentation to connect them to that place. This leads to a lifetime of searching for something tangible that they can grasp onto other than a mere feeling. In the case of CBPs, what we identify with and where we connect is generally invisible and is not bound by technicalities, official documents and legalities. The issue that arises here is that these invisible connections are just that, invisible to other people.

It is natural as a CBP to search for your identity at different stages in your life. Identity naturally changes and evolves as you experience new places and cultures and assimilate these into your life. Sometimes this occurs without you even realising that a new culture has become a part of who you are. As your identity takes on new characteristics as you experience new things you may find that you may not be fully aware that this is happening. It can be compared to when you are younger and you grow out of a pair of shoes because your feet are getting bigger as you get older. You do not notice your feet getting bigger, but they do. As a CBP your identity is growing and changing even without you realising it. It is paramount to realise that personal identity is not static and unchangeable but will change and evolve. It is a natural part of your human journey.

It is also important to realise that parents and children may not have the same perception of personal identity. When my Mum and I took our trip to Prague and began the conversations about our iden-tity, I began to dissect and analyse how my identity was not staying the same but was naturally evolving through new experiences and connections to new places. It became apparent to me that my Mum and I did not have the same perception of my personal identity. In a conversation I had with my Mum, I remember sharing with her how I felt that she had viewed my identity through her perceptions more than through my experiences. My Mum had mentioned that she never really considered that I would have a deep connection to Dubai and that this would be a big part of my identity. It is important for parents to consider and understand that a child is not born with the knowledge of their parents' past experiences in the world. A child does not know anything about the culture(s) that represent the countries shown on the passport(s) they have been issued with until they are taught about it. A child sees the world in the present. Children evolve and adapt to their surroundings as this is the natural way that humans grow. Children are not born with a knowledge and sense of identity to the country or countries they have citizenship too. It is people and parents who can sometimes think that their child will naturally connect and identify with the citizenship they are given. This is a misunderstood perception among families that have experienced living in different countries and within different cultures.

As a kid I was told that I was a New Zealander and an American and my mum purposefully created opportunities for us to learn about these two countries. It was her way to enable us to get more comfortable with who we were and how we identified ourselves. I naturally began to feel rooted in these countries because I was told that these two countries are the places I have citizenship. I assumed, and never thought differently, that this is who I am and those two countries form my identity. I was completely unaware that naturally I was developing roots in the UAE, a place that I have no legal connection to through formal citizenship. I had the right to live and go to school when I was younger in Dubai as my mum, sister and I were all issued residency visas as part of my dad's work visa. As a child I did what humans do best, I adapted to my surroundings. My identity as a child was as an American and a New Zealander out in the open yet I had no idea I was developing deep roots of belonging in the UAE. This was all to change when we set up a second home in New Zealand when I was nine years old so that my sister and I could begin to establish deeper roots in New Zealand. That is when my identity became confusing, and it changed.

When I moved to New Zealand, I was overcome with a great sense of feeling rootless. My identity as a New Zealander was different compared to the identity of New Zealanders who grew up in New Zealand. I realised my version was a version collected, perceived and influenced from being rooted in the UAE. I began to realise that I did not fit the Kiwi kid mould and that I was different. I was a different kind of New Zealander compared to my new friends in primary school. I found that we could not always relate to each other, and this was unsettling for me. Interestingly enough my best friend in primary school was a girl who was originally from England but moved to New Zealand a year before I did. We never had discussions about this rootlessness we felt as we were only children and were not at an age to analyse such concepts. What this friendship goes to show is that we as CBPs are drawn to people like ourselves because we somehow understand each other without having to discuss things in great detail.

After the move to New Zealand there was a change in me. I felt as if I did not know how to explain myself to other people. I did not realise how much Dubai was part of my identity until I left Dubai. I did not realise how different my version of a New Zealander was to other New Zealanders until I moved to New Zealand. This made me question myself as I wondered if I was even a real New Zealander. These feelings made me miss Dubai because I felt as if I belonged in Dubai more than I did in New Zealand. All these thoughts that I had were ones that I could not really explain or understand.

There is this idea about identity that assumes that there needs to be some kind of tangible representation that is written on a piece of paper to validate identity. It seems as though simply having just a feeling inside of you and a connection to a place is not enough. As I do not have any legal documentation to Dubai, I found it difficult to convince others that my identity to the UAE is a valid and honest part of who I am. Once I turned 19, I was no longer issued with a residency visa even though my dad still worked there, and our family home was still there. Despite moving to different towns in New Zealand none of them felt like home the way our home in Dubai felt. For me, New Zealand was never really home to me as a kid even though I was a citizen. When the coronavirus took its effect on the world my dad was given early retirement from Emirates Airlines. This meant that he would no longer work in Dubai and this meant that we lost our home that we had for over 20 years. For years after moving to New Zealand I had this idea that my claim to be from Dubai was valid as we still had a physical home there that I could go back to. I could tell people my parents lived in Dubai. I felt like that was enough validation to claim my connection to Dubai. In 2020 this all changed and my tangible connection to Dubai was gone. I thought that if my family and home were no longer in Dubai then how would I convince people, and even myself, that I am from Dubai?

Searching for your identity and discovering who you are is similar to that age-old quest to find yourself. In the past I have read posts or talked to friends that have said after a certain experience or life change they have finally found themselves. I would always sit back and think, how do you find yourself and how do you know when you have found it? This concept is similar to searching for your identity. How do you know when you have found it? Sometimes when searching for your identity it can seem as if there is no finish line. It can seem that way when you meet obstacles. These obstacles can be dealing with other people's opinions or wrestling with insecurities within yourself. Both can cause you to circle back to square one asking yourself the same questions that you started with, who am I and where am I from? Searching for your identity, and even more so, searching for validity in your identity, can make it feel as if you are trying to grasp for something and not even know what you are grasping for. The thing to recognise is that there is no finish line and there is nothing to grasp because life and identity is a journey that continues to change and evolve. You already have an identity, you are just adding and altering it as you evolve in the world through your experiences with different places and cultures. Keep in mind you are not in search of an identity you are in search of understanding the identity you already have. This is the paramount thing to realise.

Identity is what you identify with so take a moment or several moments over the course of time to pick apart why certain things resonate with you and why you identify with them. What you identify with is part of where you consider yourself to be from but it is so much more than that. It is everything about you. As you search for understanding you will begin to understand the reasons that you feel drawn to different places and cultures. You will understand more deeply how your identity is made up of a cultural blend and is not required to be just one piece as it is typically assumed to be. I expressed the importance of mindfulness in the previous chapter and it applies here too. Your identity becomes sustainable when it is first achieved from within. It is important to understand that others do not have to accept you first before you can accept yourself.

Once you gain a clear understanding of your identity you will gain confidence in who you are as a person. I encourage you to be confident in knowing that your identity is not a result of a weird or abnormal life. Have confidence in your identity regardless of what others perceive of you. Understand that people cannot see your internal connections, influences and memories. Keep the mindset that what other people perceive about you has to do with their exposure to the world and of culturally blended ways of life. Remain confident in the fact that you are the owner of your identity. It is in this way that you will ensure that other people's perceptions of you will not make you feel as if you have to change in order to fit in.

With all this being said, there still can remain a desire to have this invisible identity known to others. It is natural to have this strong desire to make your internal identity be expressed on the outside. As a Culturally Blended Person you can have deep connections to places and cultures that you are not always recognised for, especially in terms of technicalities and legalities, yet you want to be recognised for it. Here is an example of how I have creatively achieved putting my internal identity on the outside so I can proudly represent my unique and meaningful cultural blend.

In March of 2017, I was in Wellington, New Zealand. I had begun applying for my working holiday visa for Canada for the 2017/18 winter season. I was gathering my New Zealand documents, filling out forms, making photocopies, as well as, contemplating the idea of renewing my USA passport. I thought that since I will be in British Columbia, Canada, I could pop over to the USA and see my family in Washington State. I noticed something that I had already known but never really recognised the significance of before. I have two separate birth certificates, two separate passports and two separate SSN/IRD numbers, one from New Zealand and one from the United States. Everything is separate but I do not feel separate. Upon further contemplation I realised that I feel like a blend of three countries. The legal documentation that I was holding did not even take into account Dubai. I realised in that moment that I have no piece of paper that connects me to the place I spent the early developmental years of my life. I realised on that day, in March of 2017, that there is actually not one document that I hold that has all three of the countries that I connect to written down with my name on it. At that very moment, I grabbed a piece of paper and I wrote the initials of these three countries down, all in a row, and all connected to each other.

U.A.E.U.S.A.N.Z

This written representation of me, of my identity, was very symbolic to me and I felt that it offered closure. I knew right then and there that I wanted it to be permanently part of me because the combination of these three places is where I feel that I am from each in their own individual ways but still side by side. A few weeks later I got a tattoo that reads U.A.E.U.S.A.N.Z. It was as if the internal identity of me was now externally seen and visible on the outside. This tattoo is very symbolic to me because it represents who I am. I am a combination, a special brew of cultures, that would not conventionally go together but they do from my perspective. My tattoo represents my internal view of myself that I can now forever display on the outside. Each person deserves to have the confidence in identifying with their own unique collaboration of countries and cultures too.

I encourage you to do something creative with your own unique identity. It is an act of putting the inside on the outside which is symbolic and soulful. You do not have to have it tattooed on your body to make it significant. The significant part is that you create a way to offer closure by putting the inside on the outside. You can use the initials idea that I have done and get it engraved on a piece of jewellery. Alternatively, you can make it into an art project such as a painting or carve it into a piece of pottery. There are endless options for you to explore.

I am not the only one who has done something like this. I have mentioned before that humans naturally resonate, identify and become influenced by their surroundings regardless of citizenship, physical attributes and assumed cultures. I have a friend of mine who spent two years in the United Kingdom on her OE, the Kiwi term for an overseas experience. She had the outline of the UK tattooed on her arm. Those two years in the UK were significant to her in the evolving formation of her identity. Another friend of mine immigrated to Australia and had the outline of Australia tattooed on her arm after forming a special bond with Australia, invisible but real. Another friend of mine was born in Australia but was adopted by New Zealand parents and had the outline of New Zealand tattooed on his arm. Tattoos are permanent so the fact that myself and others in similar circumstances have a desire to make our identity permanent is monumentally symbolic. It is accompanied with a sense of pride and it goes to show just how important our unique way of belonging is to us.

To tie all of this together, it is important for you to come to terms with the realisation that the mould you feel that you need to fit into does not work for a CBP. It is important for Culturally Blended People to perceive the mould as malleable. I started this deep dive sharing with you about a girl that I met in Canada outside the ski shop who felt like she had no identity. The reality is that she does have an identity and it is unique to her. She identifies with Australia and she believes she is from Australia, despite what her New Zealand passport says. Her identity, again, is so much more than legalities and technicalities and she does not need to validate it with official documents, as long as, she achieves confidence in her unique way of belonging. Your identity is much like the Astronomical Clock's hourly performance. It is made up of individual parts moving in their own way yet fluidly working simultaneously together to create an eye-catching performance. Your identity is a collection of multiple experiences and connections in your life that are all individual, yet they all work together. You are never in search for your identity as if you do not have one, you are just in search to understand the identity you already have.

Lorraine's Deep Dive of

SEARCH FOR IDENTITY

A PERSON'S LIFE story is not merely a biography of the facts and events of their life but it is the way a person interprets those facts and events into who they are. Research has shown that it is not just the things that happen to us that define who we are but how much we have made sense of what has happened to us. We form our identity from the experiences that we have and with the groups and communities that we are involved in. In the case of Culturally Blended People, we combine our experiences that we have in different cultural and national settings and weave these together into our own personal story. This becomes our narrative, our identity story. Not all stories are simple. Many are detailed which is often the case with Culturally Blended People. Studies show that people that make sense of their life story and how it is woven together and connected have a greater sense of well-being.

Research shows that people are not compiling their life stories from birth. The ability to create a life narrative takes a little while to happen and does not begin to happen the moment we are born. The natural human developmental process at a very young age gives priority to things like walking, talking and other life skills. At that stage in life, young children tell stories about isolated events, but they do not yet weave these stories together and seek to make sense out of them. It is in the late teens and early years of adulthood that story construction really picks up. At this stage of natural human development people have cognitive tools mature enough that reinforce the natural human ability to create a coherent life story. Knowing this it is not surprising that Ashley's questions about her identity and how to tell her story did not surface until later in her life. Her recognisable search began in her early twenties and was most notably voiced during the week we spent in Prague. At that time Ashley was 20 years old and was at the normal stage of human development to want to find the answers of her identity. She wanted to know how to weave her experiences together to define her identity for herself. The many conversations that were initiated in Prague and continued long after became the core content of this book. One of the key purposes of this book for me is to bring awareness to the fact that children that grow up in and among different cultures will struggle with their identity and may not be able to make sense of this. As they approach their late teens and early twenties they will need people who will listen, offer support, and assist them as they find their way to tell their own identity story.

As I reflect on my daughters as young children and their subsequent movement into their teenage years I recognise now that I missed a key part of Ashley's formation of her identity. I now recognise, thankfully to the conversations that I have had with Ashley in writing this book, that my shortcomings were because I did not realise the core reasons that began Ashley's internal struggle with how she would define herself. I did not realise the impact that other people's comments, questions, and confusion about where she was saying she was from was internally and emotionally affecting her. These people were teachers, fellow students, friends and even family members that she encountered when she began going to school in New Zealand. I did not know because Ashley was at a stage that she was still absorbing her experiences. She was not at a stage where she could voice what the feelings of rootlessness and lack of belonging were because she had not started trying to really dive deep and understand them herself. Ashley's sense of her own personal identity, her identity narrative, was just beginning to form in her teenage years as I now understand from the research. I now see that I could have offered more support and could have been more aware. I do recognise the difficulty initiating conversations with teenagers as they are still searching for an understanding of who they are and where they belong. They are not always able to express their thoughts.

As Ashley has mentioned, the challenges in defining her identity clearly happened when she began her schooling in New Zealand at the age of nine years old. It was then, for the first time, that she was challenged with her perception of her identity as it did not match what others thought of her. Up until this time living in Dubai she had been surrounded by friends, peers, teachers, and coaches that all lived in a multicultural environment. When she was younger her identity was multicultural and blended and this was recognised and positively accepted by others. Upon arriving in New Zealand she did not have this same support and people did not recognise that her perception of her identity was not the same as the perception that they had. This is not an accusation that anyone did anything wrong. My point is that because there was no conversations and awareness available to address the issues of someone like Ashley trying to integrate into a more singular culture, Ashley was confronted to manage on her own the issues associated with her identity. As her mother I did not assist enough, her teachers were not aware of children like Ashley, her coaches did not fully understand her, and family and friends were unaware.

As I look back on the transition period of Ashley's schooling at the age of nine from Dubai to New Zealand, Ashley was at the developmental stage to view her life stories individually. She had not begun yet the deep search for her collective understanding of her identity that would be part of her developmental growth in her late teenage years. Knowing what I know now, I can understand that she was left with an internal conflict that she felt deeply and emotionally but could not explain. I always thought she was doing well. She was happy, had nice friends at school and was involved in activities that she enjoyed. In my mind, she had settled amazingly well into her transition to schooling and life in New Zealand from Dubai.

I would like to share the story of two experiences that I personally had when I moved to Dubai as a new mother in 1998 to highlight the importance of having support when we move to new places which often occurs with Culturally Blended People and their families. I believe these types of support systems are needed for young people who move with families to new countries. It is important to remember that children and teenagers are often left to figure things out on their own and integrate into a new place when families experience international moves. The reason for this is that often the place that they move has people who are simply unaware of what these children and teenagers are feeling and experiencing. These people may include extended families and certainly includes schools and groups that young people attend and become involved in.

My personal experiences that I share with you are examples of how a support system can positively affect a person who is moving into a new place. The support I received allowed me to settle into the Dubai way of life which was so foreign to me when I first stepped off the plane with a one-year-old and another baby shortly on the way. Dubai was a city in a new country that I had never lived before. I was a new mother, and my husband had a job where he was naturally away on flights for days at a time. I was left without having any family and having any friends close by. Everything was new. Coupled with that, as I soon became pregnant with my second daughter, I chose not to start work at that time. Before arriving in Dubai, I still had a strong connection to work colleagues that offered support. Once I arrived in Dubai, the first experience that occurred that offered support to me was with a group of ladies, pilot's wives, who contacted me and brought me into their circle of friendship. They knew I would need support, so they simply reached out. Suddenly I had a group of ladies who had experienced a move into Dubai like I just did that would help me through the unknowns that I would experience and soon I was able to help others. The second experience occurred with a lady that lived in the compound that we lived. Louise took me aside and personally shared strategies that she used to adjust to the newness of life in Dubai. We had conversations over coffee, conversations that I could not have with my family back in the United States or other friends in other countries as they did not understand my new situation. Louise understood and more importantly she took the time to connect through conversation. These conversations created that community feeling of belonging that assisted me greatly in my first few years in Dubai as I searched and discovered new parts to how I would perceive my personal identity that was evolving and changing with this new experience. These are two examples of support that I received upon my arrival into Dubai and these types of assistance can be replicated in other situations. I believe that with the growing number of people like Ashley moving to new countries, there should be more awareness to provide support systems for teenagers and young people to assist them as they settle in and adjust to a new environment.

As a parent I wish I would have understood what I know now. The sole reason that I have the understanding that I have now is because of the conversations that I have had with my daughter. I appreciate immensely her ability to clarify her feelings so that I can understand and look to find ways to assist others: parents, teachers, coaches, grandparents, caretakers, friends and parents of friends to be aware and to understand. We have a world full of children and young people that are growing up just like Ashley yet with their own story, their own identity narrative. They are experiencing challenges as others seek to define them on their terms. They may not yet fully understand themselves and cannot yet vocalise to others exactly who they are and where they come from. It is important that adults assist, educate, guide and converse with young people so that they can build the confidence and understanding in their own identity.

As I previously mentioned, one of the core reasons for writing this book is to bring the conversation to the forefront about how people like Ashley, Culturally Blended People, can be supported in the developmental years of their life especially in the instances where they move from a place they consider home to a place that they are told they are from, often a country that they have citizenship to. It is important that we have more conversations about this and become aware of our own actions so that we can create a better environment that is welcoming and accepting of people who define home and where they are from as a cultural blend. A person's identity is intrinsically connected to places and experiences more than to citizenship papers that place a stamp of identity as a geographical place regardless of real connection or former connections to other places.

Invisible Identity

When considering identities that are woven from a collection of experiences and cultures, as is the case with a Culturally Blended Person, it is important to understand the concept of Invisible Identity. It is important to realise that when one is searching or on a quest to discover their identity, that one's invisible identity should also be included in the search. The best way to explain the concept of Invisible Identity is to consider an iceberg. The amount of the iceberg that is visible outside of the water is 10 percent, 90 percent of the iceberg is invisible and lies under the water. Although the percentages may be different when considering the Invisible Identity of each person, the visualisation is the same.

It is a common occurrence among Culturally Blended People when they are asked the question *where are you from* to hear the response "no you are not". The reason that this happens is that when a person, me included, asks the question *where are you from* they have already begun to form the expected answer in their mind. The expected answer is drawn from what one sees and hears. People, me included, automatically assume someone is from somewhere based on the way they look or how they sound or what clothes they are wearing. Kwong Yue Yang shared two stories with me that perfectly illustrate the reality of

Invisible Identity. Kwong grew up in Australia. As a Culturally Blended Person he also connects with China. Despite the fact that he identifies with being Australian, when he is in China this is rebutted. He recalls an incident when a taxi driver in China said to him, "You can't be from Australia, you don't have blonde hair and blue eyes". As a Culturally Blended Person part of his blend was refuted. The Australian part of his identity was invisible to the taxi driver. Kwong also shares an experience when he was the one that made an incorrect perception of someone else. "I remember when I was studying in China learning Chinese and living in the foreign dormitory and I met a British born Chinese (ethnically Chinese but born in the UK). When he opened his mouth it blew my mind. I had heard the British accent on TV but only spoken by people assumed to be of Caucasian and African descent. I had met Chinese people with Australian or American accents but never had I heard a Chinese looking person with a British accent and my mind couldn't handle it." This is a perfect example of how perceptions that we have often override the reality of what is. We often do not see the Invisible Identity of a person as we only see the 10 percent of the iceberg of identity which is our perceived idea of who they are based on what we see and hear.

In my case I was born in the United States. For the first 25 years of my life I was viewed as an American. After marrying a person from New Zealand and having children that are multicultural in their own right, I naturally began to embrace a new culture that would become a distinct part of my identity, that of a New Zealand connection. This is further exemplified as in 2013 I became a New Zealand citizen and two years later I gave up my American citizenship. Legally, I am no longer an American citizen but surely that part of my iceberg is not cut off and simply left to float away from who I am and what I hold true as my identity. Ironically, the American part of me, the one that I legally have no connection to anymore, is the only part of the iceberg that is used by others to identify me. I feel that I do not really belong anywhere now. If I am in the United States or around Americans and I say that I am American the response is, "No you are not, you don't sound like one." If I say that I am from New Zealand, as that is where I now live and hold citizenship, the response is still, "No you are not, you don't sound like one." More importantly, if someone asks me *where are you from* I want to share all of me, all of the identity iceberg. I do not just want them to perceive me as 10 percent of who I am and believe that to be the only truth.

The concept of Invisible Identity can also be considered in the same way that a person who is colour-blind sees colours. My dad was colour-blind. His eyesight was 20/20 and he saw objects in clear definition. However, he physically could not see the same colours that other people saw. If he was shown a red card, he would see what many would consider an olive green. If he was shown a bright pink card he would see a dull grey. In using this analogy to better understand Invisible Identity, it is important to realise when a person who is colour-blind does not see the colour that others are seeing that this is not done intentionally. Just like colour-blindness, not all people can see the cultural blends that make up a person. A person's identity is often internal yet we usually perceive people's identity based on outward characteristics.

Everyone wants to be perceived as they perceive themselves but this is not always easy. As in the case of the colour-blind analogy, it is not the lack of wanting to see the colour accurately, it is the reality that is not possible. The only way for a colour-blind person to see with colour accuracy is to have a corrective procedure done or to invent a pair of glasses that would accurately show the colours to the colour-blind person. At the moment a procedure or an accurate pair of glasses does not exist for colour-blind people. In the same light, at the moment, there does not exist systems in place or mindsets that will accurately allow Culturally Blended People to be perceived as they want to be perceived, as a blend that makes up the whole of who they are. Will this change? Most certainly it will. It will start with a greater awareness of the issue that books like this seek to expose and through the conversations at family, school and community levels. Conversations that you will be part of and share with others.

The movie Tarzan shows a good example of how one's search for their own identity is unique to them. In the movie of Tarzan that I saw when I was younger, Tarzan ventures into the civilised world, New York City. Although he resembles the humans in the city, he finds that he does not fit in there. The reason is that although he looks human on the outside he really is from two different worlds. He is a combination of the animals in the jungle and the humans in the city. The Disney version of the Tarzan movie also depicts accurately what it feels like to search for one's identity, only to come to the conclusion that we are each our own special and unique self. In the Disney version of Tarzan II, the song by Tiffany Evans "Who Am I" voices the struggles of people that are searching for their identity. I encourage you to listen to it and relate it to the concepts in this deep dive.

Throughout the movie Tarzan II, Tarzan is a young adolescent struggling to fit in with his peers. Remember, he is a human who was raised by apes. Throughout the movie, Tarzan attempts to answer the question about his identity. He tries to act like each of his friends and fit into their world. He attempts to be an ape, a giraffe, a bird, and various other animals, only to finally realise that he is not exactly like any one of them, yet at the same time he is a human. It is important to remember that he is not only human in how he perceives his identity, but he is also a blend of all the experiences and people, or in this case animals, that create the blend of his identity. Tarzan has an internal conflict as he is not able to feel like he fits in anywhere. He does not feel fully human and he does not feel fully like each animal, he is a blend. At the end of the Disney movie, his friend Zugor answers his plea with the simple statement, "You are Tarzan". Tarzan is his own person and he has his own identity. He is a blend and he has a unique identity of his own.

Knowing how to express identity on an individual level encompasses a person's search to know why they are important. It gives validity to why their life does matter. As humans we seek to reach our full potential naturally. In order for any person to reach their potential and to be of value to those around them they have to first know who they are and have internal confidence in that. It is a personal journey that every individual should take.

PART TWO

DISCOVERING
to find out and learn

5

THE MOVE

THURSDAY IN PRAGUE
A Visit to The Zoo

Ashley

"MUM, LET'S GO." Once again, I was waiting for Mum as she found some last-minute things to do. "If you don't hurry we will miss the bus that is passing by in 10 minutes that will take us to the zoo."

We had to pick up our pace and break into a run for the last 100 metres to get on the bus. We made it but we were too late to find a seat. Holding on to the handholds in the middle of the aisle we headed out of the city. Mum always took me and my little sister to zoos when we were younger. One of my favourites was the Cheyenne Mountain Zoo near Colorado Springs in the USA where Grandma and Grandpa Tanguay lived. My second favourite one was the zoo in Singapore. When I was much younger, we would often go to New Zealand to visit Grandma and Grandad Taylor and have a day stopover in Singapore. Mum and I read about the Prague Zoo earlier that morning during our delicious European styled breakfast. We learnt that the Prague Zoo is said to be the fifth best in the world.

By the time the bus slowed down in front of the zoo we were overlooking the city of Prague that looked like a snow globe in the distance. Mum and I spent the next four hours walking around the zoo. We were amazed at the diversity of animals, birds and reptiles that inhabited this expansive place. As Mum and I were walking around the zoo we realised that it was a lot bigger than we had thought. We found ourselves taking longer stops at the foodie stalls strategically placed throughout the zoo. Mum would eyeball the dangling European sausages each time and say the same thing, "Those look exactly like the Polish sausages my Grandma Spychalla would make for us!" While I would eyeball the Nutella trdelník without any family sentiment.

At each food stall we found a wooden bench to sit at to the side of the joyful spectators. During these moments throughout the day our conversations were centred on the animals we had seen and the animals to see next. Our conversations about the animals began to blend with the *where are you from* conversations we had been having throughout the week. Despite the fact that each animal originated traditionally from a different place they were all now permanent residents of Prague. The kangaroos whose label said they are 'Australian' were probably brought over young or even bred in the Prague Zoo. We began to wonder where would the animals say they are from if they could talk. Are the kangaroos really Australian or are they European roos? We debated whether a kangaroo typically from Australia would have any sense that they are Australian because of how they look. We wondered, if the elephants that were born in the Prague Zoo were taken back to the country that their ancestors came from, would they find it easy to adjust to an environment that was not their norm. We reflected about the movement of some of the animals from different countries to the Prague Zoo and explored our joint move from Dubai to New Zealand. We compared our personal stories of moving countries and discovered things about each other's perceptions and realities that we had not discussed together until that day, 11 years after our move to New Zealand from Dubai.

Ashley's Deep Dive of

THE MOVE

IT IS OFTEN the case that Culturally Blended People have a story about a move that becomes a significant event in their life. It is when one leaves a place and goes to a new place that many of the issues for CBPs arise. In this deep dive, I will be telling my story of my move and some of the main issues that arose that you may be able to relate to. Hearing about how someone else struggles with a similar issue reminds us that we are not alone as CBPs because sometimes we can feel isolated. This can be the case when people around you do not understand you and when you feel like you do not know who to talk to about what you are experiencing. This can cause you to bottle up the feelings that you have which then become unresolved and act as a barrier when it comes to trying to define your identity, belonging, home and where you are from. Each person, each CBP, has their own story. Your story is unique to you. Your story is likely to be different from the stories of members of your family who experienced the same move as you did.

My first moving story is when I made the move from living permanently in Dubai to living in New Zealand when I was nine years old. The reason my parents chose to give my sister and I this opportunity was so that we could spend some time in our younger years living and experiencing life in one of the countries that we had citizenship to. New Zealand was to be the place that we would now go to school, Dad would visit during the school terms and every school holiday we would travel back to be in Dubai to see Dad. My mum moved to New Zealand with us first to ensure that we settled well into our new environment with the intention of moving back to Dubai once my sister and I were settled into boarding school in a few years' time.

As I share my story, I will describe the second kind of misunderstood perception that I brought up in Chapter 2. This is the misunderstood perception that you have of yourself. I will go into detail about four misunderstood perceptions that I had of myself when I first moved to New Zealand. You may be able to relate to them but keep in mind that these are not the only four that exist. Everyone will experience their own kind of misunderstood perceptions in relation to their own identity. Yours will be unique to you. This deep dive will serve as an encouragement for you to also deep dive into your own misunderstood perceptions that you may have of yourself.

I remember feeling very content and excited with this next chapter in my life. Previous holidays to New Zealand were always fun, especially staying at my grandparents' house as they had an abundance of passionfruit, feijoas and mandarins to eat. We had aunties and uncles who owned farms with all kinds of animals which we would play with when we visited. I grew up watching American/Western/English TV shows so I had this image of what kids growing up in a western society was like. The muddy green grass at school, the classrooms with chunky desks where the lid lifted up, yellow school buses and the sashes Girl Guides wore when selling cookies.

There was excitement and curiosity when it came to imagining myself living day in and day out in a western society as I thought of it. I was ready to fully experience my country. At the same time that I was preparing to leave Dubai so were many of my neighbours and friends. We were all preparing to move countries, just each going in different directions. It was common and normal in Dubai for children to return to their assumed home country as they neared secondary school either to move with their family or to attend boarding school. Within the society of expats, it was the natural and normal thing for families to do.

In June of 2006, it was so exciting arriving into the cold, rainy, occasional snow, and short days of the Southern Hemisphere from the hot, sunny and long days of the Northern Hemisphere. It was so exciting moving into a small rural town surrounded by farms that serviced the local mountain during the ski season. It was so exciting moving into our new house which looked like a typical Kiwi house. Our Kiwi house had low ceilings and mostly carpeted floors unlike the high ceilings and tiled floors in our Dubai home. It was so exciting going to the local Postie Plus store with my sister to get our new school uniforms. We traded our plaid dresses and straw hats for skorts (shorts that looked like a skirt), thick stockings and fleece jackets. It was both nerve-racking and exciting starting our first day at our new primary school. We traded our drive down the road alongside identical connected villas in Dubai to walking along footpaths where every house on the street was different. As we neared the school, we traded walking past peacocks and chickens in Dubai to passing this one fat woolly sheep. We traded turf for real grass and palm trees for big, dark green trees. We traded a modern and large school for an older, smaller country school. I walked into my new classroom which was carpeted and arranged with rows of chunky desks where the lid lifted up unlike the tiled floors and communal desks in Dubai. It was everything I had imagined and hoped that my new life in New Zealand would be like.

I was only gathering experiences at this point. I was beginning to recognise when different things seemed weird or normal to me, but I was only nine, so I was not putting a reason and connection behind these differences. What I did not realise was that the expectation I had was going to be significantly different to the reality I was soon to experience. I always thought of myself as a New Zealander but after the initial settling in period in New Zealand I was forced to face reality. I realised I had to play nine years of catch up as my understanding of New Zealand was formed while I lived in a different country. I was now living and going to school with children who had spent every day of the past nine years living and going to school in New Zealand whereas I had not. The New Zealand that I thought I belonged to suddenly began to feel a bit foreign. I was not expecting this.

The first misunderstood perception that you can have of yourself is that you think you will automatically be considered a local in the country that you have citizenship.

I always considered myself a Kiwi kid through and through. Upon my arrival in New Zealand in 2006, I began to quickly realise that I was nine years behind on general things that Kiwi kids knew. I was constantly asking my friends what this was and what was that. I would ask questions like why do we do this and how do we say that? Most of the time that I asked such questions, trying to learn about this place I was meant to belong to, I would get a face peering back at me with a questioning, confused look as they thought I already knew these things. It was these reoccurring incidents that caused me to feel like a hidden immigrant even though I technically was not an immigrant. I have New Zealand citizenship but in reality, I was immigrating into a whole new society. This was something that neither my mum nor I predicted.

Not only did I have nine years of catching up to do but I was making friends with people who had known each other since kindergarten. My Dubai hometown friends were all over the globe and I did not know at the time that I was unlikely to ever see them again. All the friends I was making in New Zealand had people around them that they had grown up with for their whole life, except me. They all had these memories with each other, except me. As I grew up and moved to different places in New Zealand, I started to feel as if I was really missing out on a lot of things that were so standard for everyone around me to have. I did not have a hometown in New Zealand like everyone else and I did not have the hometown group of friends to go with it. This introduced a feeling of loss. It was as if I did not have something I should as everyone else had it and it started to make me feel detached from New Zealand. It made me feel as if I was not a real New Zealander and not a local because I was different.

This was a perplexing realisation to have as I had always felt as if I would be considered a local in New Zealand until I moved to New Zealand. This is a concept that many CBPs that I have spoken to have said that they can relate to. I felt more like a New Zealander in Dubai than I did in New Zealand. This was a bizarre reality to get my head around. How could this be? The feeling of being a hidden immigrant endured and several people still to this day think that I am not a real New Zealander. This introduced a feeling of rootlessness as if I was hovering over the world not knowing where I could touch down as in each place there seemed to be a reason why I could not be a local in the traditional sense. I soon realised that I could never fit the mould of a normal Kiwi because I did not grow up in New Zealand. I felt different from my New Zealand classmates and friends. After some time, I began to resent the lifestyle my family had chosen for us. These thoughts and perspectives that I developed shadowed all the important values, experiences and memories I had gained throughout my culturally blended way of life. I did not truly appreciate the opportunity that I had as a young child growing up in a place like Dubai. The primary school that I went to in Dubai had children from 35 different countries. Cultures blending was a common part of my growing up years. I never knew anything different. It was so normal to have an openness and understanding of different countries and cultures. Yet, when I moved to New Zealand, I left all this behind and the only thing I began to focus on was wanting to fit in and to just be a regular run-of-the-mill Kiwi kid. I now know that I neglected the things that I should have been so grateful for. I also now realise that many of the people that I met in New Zealand had never met someone like me. I shared that I felt as if people did not understand me, but I now realise it was not a deliberate act on anyone's part. The main point I want to make is that it is in each of us to value ourselves first and to celebrate the cultural blend that we are as a unique and special identity. We cannot always expect others to understand or empathise with our situations.

I did not realise then that being a local of a country and fitting into the traditional mould was not as important or necessary as knowing and valuing my own special and unique qualities and characteristics that my culturally blended life offered to me. Often it can feel as if it is so important to be like everyone else because you just want to fit in and not stick out like a sore thumb. You cannot be something that you are not. The only way to resolve the internal conflict that comes from not valuing who you are is to realise that no one is the same. You can only value yourself and build confidence in your culturally blended way of life when you stop comparing yourself to others and do not focus on what you think you have missed out on. You can be a local of a country important to you in your own definition, it does not have to be based on what the traditional definition is. This is the mindset that you need to embrace on your own. You can do this by beginning with having respect for your culturally blended life and all the value and important perceptions you have because of it.

The second misunderstood perception that you can have of yourself is that you are going back home to a country you have citizenship to when in reality you have only lived in that country briefly or never at all.

I always thought that moving to New Zealand was perceived as myself and my family going back home. The conversation that I heard my parents have with our family friends in Dubai was always, "We are taking the kids back home." It was an expectation I had that I would fit into the New Zealand way of life like a glove because it was my home country. The move to New Zealand did not eventuate like I thought it would. I was to come to understand after the conversations that I had with Mum in Prague that she was not going home either. Mum was starting the formal process of immigrating to New Zealand.

It was not clear to me at first, but in 2006 I boarded the plane in Dubai to head off to my motherland, but I left my homeland behind in the UAE. Going to New Zealand, as I came to find out, was not going back to anywhere that I previously had a life. I realise now that this term 'going back' was not my words but were the words I heard my parents and my friends' parents in Dubai use. The ironic part of this misunderstood perception is that my dad, the New Zealander, was staying in Dubai to work so he was not technically going home. He was staying in Dubai, and we would now have two homes to create the best situation for my family. The other ironic part is that my American mother was the person introducing us to the New Zealand way of life even though she actually never lived in New Zealand before. From my mum's perception, New Zealand felt like home to her since marrying my dad and having my Kiwi grandparents welcome her into the family. New Zealand felt like home to her in a way but despite what was thought, the reality was that my mum, sister and I were all immigrating into a new society. We were not going back home as we never had a life there to go back to. This is a common misunderstood perception that many people and families have when making their decision to go back, so to speak, to their country of citizenship or to the country of citizenship of one parent. This perception veiled the problems we could never have foreseen in terms of defining home.

It is important to be aware in the case of families moving that each family member will have a different perception of home. This can introduce frustration and tension which is the result of misunderstood perceptions. My mum was trying to make New Zealand our new home, I soon came to realise that Dubai felt more like home than New Zealand did. When we first moved to New Zealand, we spent every school holiday during primary school going back to Dubai. This changed when I started secondary school as during the third term school holiday, we would stay in New Zealand so that we could go skiing as a family. My dad, who was still living and working in Dubai, would get that time off work so that he could spend two weeks with us in New Zealand. I remember that school holiday each year spent in New Zealand was not the same kind of happy holiday as the ones when we were in Dubai. I missed the heat, the pools, the beaches, the lifestyle, the food and most of all I missed being in my house in Dubai because that felt the most like home to me. I liked New Zealand for school, but I never wanted to spend more time than I had to in New Zealand because I always had this underlying feeling of homesickness. I deeply missed Dubai. I started to resent the home my mum was trying to make for us in New Zealand because I felt as if my parents were trying to replace Dubai. I got into arguments and got frustrated with my parents because of this and it was viewed as being a moody teenager. From my mum's perspective, she was trying to make New Zealand feel like home to us because it is our country of citizenship and she was trying to facilitate that connection for us. It was important to her to make us feel grounded in a place that we were meant to belong. In addition to that my dad wanted to spend his holidays in New Zealand because this is where he grew up and feels most like home to him. We each had different perceptions of home and they were not necessarily aligned with each other. It was only after the trip to Prague, and the conversations that began there, that my mum really began to understand my thoughts and perceptions.

The more I experienced conflict of where I belonged and where home was meant to be, the more I felt like a foreigner in my own country. As I grew up my family moved to a few different homes and towns within New Zealand. This resulted in me feeling as if nowhere was a hometown for me in New Zealand. We moved each time for good reasons, yet it created this growing unpleasant feeling in me where I was struggling to feel that I truly belonged anywhere. This made me feel constantly different from anyone else. I felt not relatable to other Kiwi kids. This is not the best feeling to have when trying to fit into a place you are supposed to belong. The feeling of missing home is a very powerful emotion especially when it is accompanied by the feeling that you do not belong in a place that is supposed to be your home, based on a piece of paper.

As I began to try to understand the instances that happened that caused the conflicts I experienced in the move to New Zealand, I became aware of how I could have reacted and absorbed the situations that were presented to me. I perceived New Zealand as going back home and that was the misunderstood perception my family had. This made it seem like I would just fit in which I did not because I was different, I had a completely different childhood to the New Zealanders in New Zealand. The New Zealand way of life was foreign to me, it was not home to me until I became accustomed to it years after moving. My family should have treated the move to New Zealand in recognising that I was a hidden immigrant. Before actually moving to New Zealand, New Zealand was never in fact an actual home, it was just where I came for holidays a couple times and held citizenship. When I moved to New Zealand, I was not going home I was in fact discovering a new society. This is the reality for many CBPs, and it is very normal for us. We just need different kinds of coping and healing tactics when faced with this situation because it does not have to be a situation which fuels ongoing homesickness. I realise now that I did not have to perceive that calling New Zealand home was in anyway me having to give up or replace my home in Dubai. I could have viewed it as just growing a connection with a new place. Yes, I was in a sense, losing something but I was also gaining something new. As a Culturally Blended Person you become the blend of the places that you connect to regardless of whether you are physically there or not. This is the key to understanding the cultural blend of who you are as a person. As I began to view my move to New Zealand in this way my misunderstood perception transformed into a new perception of not losing a home but gaining a new one while still always having the old one part of who I am. This is the way I now see the world, how I live my life, and what I find comfort in. It can be difficult at first when you feel as if you have lost something, but you must realise that you never truly lose anything that is part of who you are. It is true that you might not physically be in a place that you are culturally connected to but that does not mean that those cultures and places leave you. They are part of you. They are woven into your blend. Home has to be recreated wherever you are, and it has to live inside of you. You have to blend those homely connections you have into your current situation so that it feels alive in your day-to-day life.

The third misunderstood perception you can have about yourself is thinking that other people think like you do which can lead to a difference in perception of what is weird and what is normal.

Differences of what is considered weird and normal in different places can sometimes be a shock to the system. Sometimes going somewhere new or old, after a long time away from it, can make you question things and make you feel like an outcast. I experienced this when I first moved to New Zealand because from my perception the things I had and the society I lived amongst, especially the religious aspect of Dubai, seemed normal to me. I never thought twice or questioned things in Dubai despite being a New Zealander and an American. What I thought was normal when I lived in Dubai was con-sidered different and sometimes weird to the friends that I had in New Zealand. What I did not realise as a child was that I was learning about who I was as a New Zealander influenced by a society not associated with New Zealand's culture or way of life. This is where the cultural blend and misunderstood perception of myself began.

The reason for these stark differences is simply related to what one has been exposed to which is not something I thought about as a nine-year-old. Not having this perception of my own upbringing and other people's upbringing, to allow for a more helicopter point of view, is what made me become detached from the real New Zealand. This is a feeling that endured for many years. This concept is something you may be able to relate to.

Below are some of the main conversations, comments and thoughts I had about the misunderstood perceptions of what is weird and normal when I moved to New Zealand that stirred confusion into the pot of my identity and made me question who I was and where I belonged.

I felt misunderstood when people would constantly ask me where in the States I was from. I thought to myself, why am I not being recognised as a New Zealander in New Zealand when all throughout my childhood I thought of myself as both a New Zealander and an American? I would reply to people that questioned my accent and say, "I am American, but I have never lived there, I am a New Zealander too as I have dual citizenship". People would sometimes frown and would mention something about how the way I talked was not like the way New Zealanders talked. It made me feel that I did not belong in New Zealand as I thought I did.

I can distinctly remember feeling misunderstood when I would mention that my family had a maid in Dubai. People would frown and comment about how rich I was. In Dubai it is normal to have a maid and especially for my family as my dad would be away from home on international flights for days at a time. The situation my mum was in meant that it was a great help to her to have someone that we could trust and call on when needed as my mum was raising my sister and I often on her own most of the time. This is not any different from having a babysitter or even having grandparents or other family members assist as occurs in New Zealand. It was apparently weird in New Zealand to have a maid and it was viewed as a rich person thing. I did not like how my family was being perceived by the kids in New Zealand. I was perceived as someone who was spoilt due to the fact that we had a lady that assisted us and I did not understand why they thought that because in Dubai it was normal. I didn't speak about having a maid very often, but it seemed to be something that others just kept bringing up.

I felt misunderstood when I would recall memories of my life growing up in Dubai and share them with my friends in New Zealand because people would tell me to stop boasting. I did not understand the perception people had of Dubai as being this rich and glamorous place because to me it was just home. I never told my friends to stop boasting when they talked about what they did at home in New Zealand, so I did not understand why they did this to me when I talked about my home as being in Dubai. I realised later on in life that I was talking so much about Dubai to my new friends in New Zealand because I was missing it and I did not want it to disappear. I wanted to continue to recall memories of my childhood in Dubai when my Kiwi friends would recall memories of their life in New Zealand. What I found when I talked about my memories of Dubai was that kids in New Zealand could not relate to what I was saying and this put me in the position of feeling different, weird and not relatable. If you have ever felt like a hidden immigrant, a term that refers to moving to your country of citizenship but feeling like you are immigrating due to the stark differences, then you will know how foreign it can make you feel.

I felt misunderstood when I was asked questions about what it was like growing up in an Islamic society as the questions were generally negative and people assumed it was an overly conservative and oppressive culture. I would tell people that my experience was very relaxed in Dubai due to the large expatriate influence, yet there was still respect for the Islamic expectations such as covering your knees and shoulders as well as not eating in public during Ramadan. For me this was normal. It was normal to abide by this respectful code of conduct as a non-Muslim in an Islamic society, yet it was weird compared to the lifestyle New Zealanders had growing up in New Zealand.

I felt misunderstood when I would tell people that my dad was still working in Dubai while my mum, sister and I moved to New Zealand. It was not unusual in Dubai to have the mother and kids move to another country while the father stayed to work in Dubai. As an international pilot, my dad was more often away from Dubai on a flight than he was in Dubai. For other families in this situation, of one parent based in Dubai but not present in the country for much of the time, it made sense to set up a second home in a country of the family's citizenship. Dubai is considered a transient society from an expatriate point of view in that people are there to work. It is common for people to live and work there for a few years and then leave. Expatriates that live in Dubai are not able to immigrate and become citizens of Dubai. Despite this being so normal in Dubai, it was so strange and weird for the people I met in New Zealand. Sometimes other kids in New Zealand would comment to me that the reason I am in New Zealand is because my parents were getting divorced. If I tried to explain that this was not true, they would frown and tell me that it was suspicious and weird. I never thought that us moving to New Zealand was weird until the comments from others were made. When the kids in New Zealand would tell me that my parents were getting divorced it really unsettled me to the point that I became very anxious. I would cry to my mum about how her and dad were getting a divorce and she would never understand where I was getting that idea from. We talked to Dad all the time on Skype, and we always saw him when he flew into New Zealand and when we went to Dubai. My parents had a good relationship and always got along well. Somehow though the comments from the kids in New Zealand were louder in my head and I began to believe them and did not believe my parents. It was a horrible feeling and it made me feel as if I was so very different from everyone else which made me wonder if I was a real New Zealander.

All of these differences regarding what was weird and normal left me wondering if maybe my life in Dubai was weird. As a result of this I stopped telling people about my life in Dubai because I did not like walking away from conversations feeling weird as this always led to a growing emptiness inside of me. As a teenager, I just wanted to fit in and feel like a real New Zealander like everyone else. Despite this, I also knew that hiding who I truly was only bottled up these unresolved feelings. The questions of where home is, where am I from, what is my identity, and why do I feel like a hidden immigrant endured for a long time. It was not until I was 20 and my mum and I took the trip to Prague that the conversations started, the deep dives began and a true understanding of who I am began to make sense.

What I realise now, and want to share with you, is that the concept of something being weird or something being normal is dependent on what someone has been exposed to. I have come to realise that this type of misunderstanding can happen even when children move within a country, for example, when children move from a city to a rural area or vice versa. They too can feel as though they are different and don't belong. Becoming influenced by what other people say to the point of changing yourself comes down to your confidence in who you are, your identity, and way of life. Changing how you answer questions or even telling white lies about who you are because you think that will help you fit in better is not a solution that will give you confidence in your culturally blended self. If you do this it just becomes a band-aid to the problem. You need to see the value in your culturally blended life so that you can achieve confidence and own it. Not everyone will understand that you are a blend. However, there are certainly people that will or are at least open to expanding their own knowledge and are interested in another opinion. It is your choice to decide if a conversation with someone is worth having. This is the power you hold. You can either keep the conversation going or move onto something else. Having other people frown at you or question you is not worth your time. It is not worth feeling that you are being unpicked before your eyes to the point that you walk away from a conversation not feeling whole or feeling like you do not fit in. It is important to have the mindfulness that there are different kinds of normal and that people have been exposed and taught different things. Other people's opinions are not the decider of who you are especially in terms of your culturally blended identity.

The fourth misunderstood perception that you can have is to assume that what you have you will always have. I had this perception that what I had in Dubai, at a certain period of my life, would continue to be accessible to me as my life evolved.

When we were living in Dubai, my mum, sister and I would always take at least two trips a year to the USA to see family. Our dad would join us for a couple weeks when he got leave and we would go camping and exploring all throughout the Rocky Mountains in Colorado. After arriving in New Zealand in 2006 we went back to the United States as a family only once in 2010. The next time I went back to the United States for two weeks was when I was living in Canada in 2018 and that was it. Visiting the USA was a big part of my life when I was younger when we were living full-time in Dubai. I connected to my American citizenship, the family in the United States and the culture. America was part of who I was and how I defined myself. When we moved to New Zealand those trips stopped. The reason for this was that as we were living in New Zealand we spent our regular school holidays going back to Dubai to see our dad. I started to resent New Zealand because I had to give up something I did not want to give up. I wanted to continue to have access to visiting my grandparents in their house in Colorado, being able to visit my other family around the country, and simply being able to live in America for a time each year as that was part of who I am. I never thought that when we began living in New Zealand that the trips back to Colorado would end. As a child I resonated with the United States, and I never realised how much I related my identity to it until I did not have it anymore.

Years later I would experience this same disconnection to Dubai. Something I have mentioned already throughout this deep dive is that the more I settled into New Zealand the more I realised how much less time I got to spend in Dubai. This made me miss Dubai. I began to resent New Zealand because it just did not feel like home as much as Dubai did. In saying that, I did not want to leave New Zealand as I liked my high school, however, I did not want to spend any more time in New Zealand than I had to. I did not realise then that who I am, where I am connected to and my identity were not found in only one geographical place. I felt like I was being torn apart but I could not yet fully express this. During my first year of university I was only able to go back to Dubai once for a week and the following years I only went back to Dubai for one trip. Since Covid-19 took its effect on the world I have not been back to Dubai since 2018. During the coronavirus pandemic my dad lost his job in Dubai and our home of over 20 years went with it. I have moments of sadness because I cannot go home to Dubai. I do not know when I will be able to get back to Dubai. When I do get the chance to go back things will be different. I miss so many things about Dubai. I miss the beaches, culture and lifestyle, all those places that I have so many memories and were such a big part of me when I was growing up. These things seem so far away now that I am in New Zealand, still unable to travel freely.

Recognising these feelings and understanding them brings me to wanting to share what I have learned with you. Living a life of missing or wanting what you once had can lead to regret, grief and homesickness. These feelings add a tone of negativity to your life which do not benefit you. What I did not realise when I had these feelings was that it was completely normal. The reality is that change is a constant part of life. Even if you stay in one place forever, things, people and life will change. No one is ever exempt from these feelings regardless of if they have lived a culturally blended life or not. What I did not realise is that with every choice or change in life there is a gain and a loss. Sometimes the loss may not be important and sometimes it may be incredibly important. Always remember that during the challenging times of change, you may not see how everything fits together and how things do work out until you are past the point of change. You will also benefit from change by becoming a stronger character, growing your skills as a person, getting to experience a new place, getting a better job, having new opportunities to enjoy or maybe even having more compassion because you now understand more than one perspective. The list is endless and is dependent on your personal situation. It is important to focus on the things that you have gained during times of change even though it can be easier to focus on what you have lost. If you focus on what is gone then you will not notice the new rays of light shining in your life. The feelings of regret, grief and homesickness that come with change need to be transformed so that they serve you in a positive way. It has to be a creative task you spend time thinking about to transform your thoughts in a way that works for you. Thinking about the things you do have in the moment is what you should spend your time thinking about. Those thoughts are what should be the main undertone of your life. Your happiness will become brighter when you are able to transform your mindset during times of change.

As I finish this deep dive, I want to emphasise that moving some- where new is hard and it requires a lot of courage to do as change is hard. I shared the details of my move to be a motivation for you to explore your own move as it will be different from mine. Your move might be to a different part of the same city, within the same country, or to a new country. The commonality is that we can relate to some, or all, of the same misunderstood perceptions, concepts and feelings. For those that experience a culturally blended way of life it is important to remember that it is normal to feel different and isolated as you try to find your place. It can be difficult to find the right people to talk to and to find people that understand the issues that you are dealing with because of a move, especially if it is to a place that is supposed to be your home according to your citizenship status. People may not be able to relate to you, they may say things that hurt you. For me it is like trying to understand pregnancy. I know people that are pregnant, but I cannot really understand them as I have never been pregnant. It is pregnant women who need to talk to, ask for advice and confide in other pregnant women for the most optimal support and guidance because pregnant women are the only ones who can really know what it is truly like to be pregnant. This is a metaphor for a culturally blended way of life. It is important to feel supported, understood and know that there are other people like yourself and to seek out other people or groups who are in the same boat who know exactly what it is like. It is important to also remember that my mum and I have one viewpoint and this book is a conversation where both of our viewpoints are shared. It is to inspire others to continue the conversation, for you to share your thoughts and experiences so that greater understanding will be achieved. I encourage you to analyse any moves that you have had, especially if you feel as if you still have unresolved feelings. Putting a name to the feelings is a therapeutic way to begin to transform the feelings you do not quite understand into more clarity and to be at peace with your special unique blend.

Lorraine's Deep Dive of

THE MOVE

THE CONVERSATIONS THAT Ashley and I had at the Prague

Zoo, triggered by contemplating the big moves the animals had made, continued after we left Prague. It is often upon reflection of events in our lives that we discover the meanings and lessons woven into our journey.

The moment that I knew that it was time to offer our daughters an opportunity to live in one of the countries that they had citizenship to happened at 1 a.m. in the morning in Dubai in February 2006. Wayne's alarm went off. He sprung out of bed and headed for the shower. The flight he was rostered for was leaving in a couple of hours to Nairobi, Kenya. It was not a long flight, for international standards. He would be back in a couple of days. The alarm had not woken me up as I had not yet gone to sleep. We had come back from an enjoyable early dinner with friends the day before. They were friends whom we had known in Dubai for years and whom our children played and went to school with together. The conversations the previous evening included topics about schooling in Dubai. It was normal then that many students when they reached secondary school age would go to boarding school, often in Europe, Australia or New Zealand.

Another part of the conversation that I engaged in with my friends the previous evening was the length of time that we each had lived outside our countries of citizenship. I had left the United States for a planned two years in 1987. That two years extended indefinitely. I was now one year short of living outside of my home country for 20 years. Twenty years had gone by and there was something that was starting to bother me. I did feel as though I had a home in Dubai as that is where I was raising my children. Yet, there was this overwhelming feeling that I was now without a real home, a place that I really belonged. The home that I grew up in Colorado, the place that for many years I said I was from, was now feeling very distant. Wayne and I had always spoken about living and making a home in New Zealand. The reason that we had not done so as of yet was because Wayne's job as a captain with Emirates required that he live in Dubai.

It is important for me to share as part of my story the reason that I felt so comfortable in setting up a home in New Zealand for our family in 2006 even though I had never lived there. It is not my home per se but for 16 years I felt as though I belonged there. The day that Wayne and I got married in my hometown in the United States in 1990 was the day that his parents welcomed me with open arms into their family. On that day, I felt that I belonged to two places, USA and New Zealand.

Since our wedding day, I had made many trips to New Zealand, firstly with Wayne, and then with Wayne and our daughters. Throughout the time we spent in New Zealand, year after year, Wayne's parents always made me feel as if I belonged there, that it was my home too.

Below I share my story of the twists and turns that our move to New Zealand took. It is important to emphasise that when such moves take place we are often so busy with adapting and coping that it is years later that we are able to begin to make sense out of what happened. This is certainly the way it was for me. It was years after I made this move, spawned by the conversations in Prague, that I began to discover the lessons and meanings in my journey.

One of the characteristics of a place like Dubai is that it is very transient. People come and go as work contracts end and new opportunities elsewhere are offered. The good friends that I had made in the first years in Dubai were now beginning to drift away. Most importantly, as Ashley would soon be leaving her primary school to attend secondary school, it was obvious that she would soon be disconnected from many of her friends. Some would go to boarding school in other countries. Others would choose among a selection of secondary schools in Dubai to attend, each moving off on their own pathway. This was an ideal time to make a move.

So why was I still awake that early morning when Wayne got up at 1 a.m.? The conversations during the dinner we shared with friends the night before about where our children would go to secondary school and where we felt we had a home were still churning in my mind. When Wayne finished his shower and was getting ready to leave, I asked him a question. "What do you think if the holiday home we are building in New Zealand in the South Island was to become a more permanent home?" Carefully detailing my reasoning, I continued, "You fly often to Christchurch on regular scheduled Emirates flights. We will still come back to Dubai for the school holidays including the long summer holiday in December and January for the southern hemisphere summer. You can spend your holidays in New Zealand during the girls school time." Wayne always has and continues to be someone who is very open and understanding to my needs as a person. Picking up his captain's bag he said, "Sounds interesting. I am sure we can look into that." Just before I fell asleep, I sensed there was going be a big change ahead, a big move, and there was this happy feeling that I felt that I was going home, a home I felt that I always had since the day I got married. I was excited for what was ahead.

The next two days that Wayne was in Nairobi were busy for me. Once the girls were dropped off at school, I set to work searching on the internet to research and gather the details I needed to consider making a move like this work. I emailed the local school where the house we were building was located. I confirmed that the girls would be able to start school in a couple of months and found out where to buy the school uniforms. I got quotes from freight companies on moving items that we would need in our second home in New Zealand. Most importantly, I asked Ashley and her sister what they thought of the idea.

I had brought up the idea of the move with the girls and we had a great conversation. Later that day Ashley gave me a letter that she wrote (I still have that letter). It was a very special letter listing all the reasons that she really wanted to go to New Zealand, a place she considered her home. It was natural that she had a deep desire to connect further with her heritage and roots and to be closer to the family, especially her grandparents, that always made her, and her sister feel that New Zealand was where they belonged.

The move to New Zealand in June of 2006 was to set off a chain of events that would push me into feeling lost with a deep sense of not belonging. This was sparked by the immigration department informing me six weeks upon arriving in New Zealand that I would need to leave the country at the end of three months. A marriage of 16 years to a New Zealand citizen was not recognised, even with two New Zealand children. The reason given for this was because Wayne was still working in Dubai, even though together we owned the house we were living in in New Zealand. It meant that I had no legal right to stay living in New Zealand. My children, New Zealand citizens, could stay but I had to leave. Wayne's parents had welcomed me into their family in 1990, yet, in the eyes of the immigration department that family tie did not exist in 2006.

In just a few short weeks of settling the girls into school in New Zealand, I came to the stark reality that somehow, I did not belong in New Zealand. I remember the moment clearly. I was sitting in the local cafe having a coffee in the small town that we were living. The waitress took my order and obviously noticed an accent. "Where are you from?" she asked. It was as if an explosion that created a black hole inside of me occurred in that moment. Where was I from? Although I felt deeply connected to New Zealand, I had just been told I had to leave the country as I did not belong there, and I did not have a legal right to stay. What was worse is that I felt torn away from my New Zealand children and my New Zealand husband. Where was I from? Where do I belong? I could not be from Dubai as I was only an expat and I have never identified as being from Dubai either. I no longer felt I had a current connection to the United States and was not sure if I could really say I was solely from there anymore. It was part of my past but not of my present. The experience flashed back in my mind of the last time I went to the United States and an American said to me, "No, you are not American, you don't sound American. Where are you really from?" The question from the waitress came to me again, a bit louder this time as she had assumed I had not heard her, "Where are you from?" I had the passport, I was a citizen, I had grown up in the United States, but things had changed so much. I had not lived there for 20 years. Here I am in New Zealand with a family of New Zealanders, husband and children, yet I am not from here. The waitress realising she might have upset me asked, "Are you okay?" I smiled, "Yes I am fine, I was just thinking about something." She smiled back and went to get my coffee.

On a return visit to Immigration New Zealand to gather further information, I proceeded to move through the process of obtaining a Work to Residence Visa. This would allow me to legally stay in New Zealand. As I proceeded to move through the process of legally being allowed to stay in New Zealand, I only had myself to rely on regarding the paperwork. Again, according to Immigration New Zealand, the fact that I was married to a New Zealander and had New Zealand children had no bearing on my application for a work residency as my husband was technically a resident in Dubai. Fortunately, as a secondary school mathematics teacher with 12 years of teaching experience, my profession was on the list of people that could get a Work to Residence Visa. I was soon offered a job teaching mathematics at Mt Hutt College in Methven. My children had already started attending their new primary school which was located right next to the high school that I was teaching at. Wayne was now flying in on a regular basis with the scheduled flights that Emirates had connecting Dubai to Christchurch, New Zealand. On the surface things were working out. I was too busy to address the fact that I now felt as if I did not really belong in New Zealand. There were many things to sort and organise. The easiest thing to do was to just push my situation aside. As a mum I was focused on ensuring that my children and my family would weather any challenges. My dad raised me to make the best out of any situation and that was what I aimed to do.

A couple of years later, in 2008, after arriving and beginning to settle in the small town, we left Methven and moved north to Cambridge in the North Island. Wayne was offered the opportunity to fly the A380 and would soon be bringing the first Emirates A380 into Auckland. As Wayne would no longer be flying into Christchurch, we made the decision to move north to be closer to Auckland. When Ashley and Jennifer chose to go to boarding school in Cambridge, we shifted our family home south to be near Taupo, in the middle of the North Island. It was our move to the Taupo area that was the first time that I really felt as if I had found a home in New Zealand. The whole area reminded me of the small towns in Colorado that I always thought I would one day settle in. Taupo was nestled near the lake and ski slopes. Coincidentally, it was also near the place that Wayne grew up on the family farm, where he had moved to when he was five years old. I settled in and found that familiar homely feeling in the Taupo area. I made good friends there and began to grow roots. We have since shifted to the Christchurch area and I must say that the neighbouring town of Kaiapoi also feels like home.

What I discovered during this big move to New Zealand, and the subsequent smaller moves within New Zealand, was that each time I moved I had to find my own connection to the country. Going through the immigration process myself was an eye-opening experience for me from the initial application stage to participating in the citizenship ceremony with good friends and my family members beside me. The fact that I had to immigrate on my own and was not automatically given residency, even though I was married to a New Zealander and had New Zealand children, meant that I created my own identity with New Zealand, yet also one shared with my daughters and husband. I discovered through the years of settling into New Zealand that my identity, my sense of belonging, was something that I would be challenged with for years to come. I now had two homes, one in New Zealand and one in Dubai. As my daughters grew older, I would spend more time in Dubai. For a period of time when people would ask me *where are you from* I would simply say, "I am a twenty-first century global nomad." Today, I am a New Zealand citizen and I am no longer an American citizen. This is what the paperwork says about me. Today I no longer have a connection to Dubai physically, although it is part of the blend of who I am. I left Dubai on what I thought was a normal flight back to New Zealand in March of 2020. It is now the beginning of 2022 and I have not returned. I spent more than 20 years living in Dubai but because I was out of the UAE when the 2020 lockdowns happened, I never returned. Wayne subsequently was given early retirement meaning that our home of 20 years was now gone. As a human I have a deep desire to belong and through the years I have discovered that I belong to more than one place. My feeling of belonging is deeply connected to the United States and to New Zealand with a dash of Dubai and sprinkles of the Seychelles. My identity as a Culturally Blended Person continues to evolve. I still have times of feeling as if I do not truly belong to any one place. I find my identity in the culturally blended soil that my roots continue to grow in.

The move of 2006 as I have shared had a big impact on my identity. This move also allowed me to discover, make mistakes, and learn how to be a parent of children in this process of a major move between countries. My desire and aim as a mother when we made the move in 2006 was to ensure that my daughters would settle well into their new second home. I was focused on their adjustment and assisting them to fit in so that they could feel that they belonged to this new home we were creating. When we first moved to New Zealand and lived in

Methven, I observed the children around us and I made sure that my daughters wore what the other children wore. I made sure that they played the same sports that the other children played. I made sure that they participated in the activities that the other children participated in. It was relatively easy for me to be part of my daughter's lives in the first two years as fortunately where I was teaching was next door to Ashley and Jennifer's primary school. I was able to actively be part of the events at the school that Ashley and Jennifer were attending. I remember cheering Jennifer on during Bring a Pet Day when our imported Australian dog, Snoopy, who had lived in Dubai and was now with us in New Zealand won the obstacle race the first year. I actively supported Ashley as she played netball and Jennifer when she played field hockey. When Wayne was in town, he was able to speak to the students on Dad's Day at school. Like all the other families, on the weekends in winter we headed up to the Mt Hutt Ski Area for a cold but fun day out. As parents we were invested in ensuring that we did what we could to allow our children to thrive in their new environment and to embrace being a New Zealander as part of their birth right.

It would be years later, after the conversations that I had with Ashley in Prague, that I would begin to really understand how my daughter was finally able to process this time in her life. It was then that I would begin to process the move. It was after our conversations that I began to recognise that our world today has an exponentially growing number of people that have similar stories to ours, yet unique in their own way. I have realised that we need to do more to assist people, especially young people, who find their identity as a cultural blend. I know the struggles that are faced because I have lived it and have spent the time understanding the challenges. I have discovered that the one thing that can make things easier is if Culturally Blended People could regularly connect to and have conversations with people like themselves. Together, as we continue the conversations, we can learn from each other and not make the same mistakes and instead offer support to people who identify as being culturally blended.

6

GRIEF

FRIDAY IN PRAGUE

Einstein's Café and the Prague Castle

Lorraine

ON FRIDAY MORNING we skipped breakfast at the hotel. We had read online that a place not to be missed was Café Louvre, which we later called Einstein's Café. It first opened its doors in 1902. Albert Einstein was one of the notable and frequent guests in its early days. During the years 1911 and 1912, Einstein worked at the Prague German University. It was during this time that Café Louvre became a regular part of his stay in Prague.

The clouds were gathering as we headed out the door in a different direction than we had gone on the previous days. Walking through the streets that curved and twisted made it feel as though we were on a treasure hunt. We passed cafés, restaurants, hotels and residential buildings all squished together among the surrounding artistic buildings. I distinctly remember this iron structure of a man, hanging from an iron umbrella attached to a thin line drawn between two buildings. It was as if the male Mary Poppins was floating off into another world.

We arrived at the old building the café was located in. We walked up the stairs appreciating the items displayed on the walls detailing the cafés history. On the second floor we were welcomed by the fragrance of food into a large, elegant room. It had a high ceiling with detailed chandeliers. The curtains, tables, furniture and decorations made it feel as though we were no longer in the present day. The café was humming with smooth orchestral music, chatter from people and tings from cutlery. We were ushered to a booth next to one of the many long windows that overlooked the street below.

The waitress placed a menu in front of us. On the front was the story of the café. In an age before having conversations through the phone or via email, this cafe provided a crucial point for contacts to be made. Ideas were exchanged while people enjoyed a cup of tea or coffee throughout all seasons. It was the kind of environment that invited conversation. Our conversation stemmed from the story about Einstein that was written on the menu and the walls. While waiting for our breakfast to arrive, we searched online and found out more about Einstein including the countries that he had lived in, the countries he gained citizenship to, and the period that he was stateless. We reflected on our ancestors and friends that had taken a similar route in life of gaining and losing citizenships.

Our conversation continued until divine pastries were placed in front of us. We stopped talking while we enjoyed the flavours and textures we were tasting. As we sat silently munching away, I lapsed into deep thought. I wondered how Einstein would have answered the question *where are you from*. Would he say he was from Germany even though he renounced his German citizenship? I pondered how he would have answered this question during his years of being stateless. Einstein spent the last years of his life living in the United States and eventually gained American citizenship. I wondered if he found his identity as a cultural blend. I thought about my situation and how I also gained a new citizenship later in life and renounced my original citizenship as well. Although it was my decision to do this, nonetheless, it brought a feeling of loss. It was partly a loss of who I am, or at least the legal definition of who I am, as I no longer have citizenship to the place that I was born and for many years called home.

With our tummies satisfyingly full of delicious pastries and warm tea, we headed out of Einstein's Café to our next adventure. We caught the tram up to the Prague Castle which is said to be the largest ancient castle in the world. We walked through different areas of the castle in awe of its fairy-tale magnificence. We discovered that construction started as far back as the ninth century and has been the seat of power of a variety of kings from all eras. Amid our journey within the castle walls, we marvelled at the Basilica of St Vitus, Basilica of St George and the Golden Lane that had ancient armour built into the walls. We wandered through the Southern Garden taking a moment to lean on the mossy, smoky walls that overlooked the sloping Lesser Town.

As the day progressed the clouds started to grow more grey and a light drizzle was felt on our faces. We continued to wander. We walked through the Black Tower gate into the St Wenceslas vineyard. The drizzle turned to a more persistent patter of rain. To our pleasant surprise we spotted a garden restaurant in the distance. The restaurant was fashioned as a long porch that was sheltered by overhanging vines perched at the top of the sloping vineyard. As we ducked under the shelter of the restaurant we gazed at the expansive view of the city. We could see all the way to the Charles Bridge and all the monuments nestled together that were misty in the rain showers, now tiny in perception. It was as if we were looking into a snow globe. We took our place at a little square dining table and, as had become customary on our trip to Prague, we ordered two frothy beers to accompany us as we waited out the rain.

The dampening rain also dampened our mood and created a twist, a new angle, to our conversation about *where are you from*. This melancholy atmosphere moved us to conversations about grief. We recounted our feelings of when we moved from one place to another and how we felt a sense of loss that we now recognised as grief. Although grief is typically associated with the loss of a person usually through death, it is a feeling that is transferrable to any loss that one experiences. As the rain grew heavier so did our conversation. We uncovered and shared the losses that we had both felt moving countries, belonging, identity and trying to understand where we were from when it felt like we were from nowhere. On this rainy day in Prague, we unveiled stories that neither of us had heard from each other before. We learned more about each other and a bit more about ourselves underneath the vines, sheltered from the rain.

Ashley's Deep Dive of
GRIEF

GRIEF IS A response to a loss, a loss that can be experienced in all corners of life, not just when you have lost a loved one. In the case where a sense of loss is felt that is not connected to losing a person, grief can be unexpected and undetected. Up until my mum and I had a conversation about this under the vines in Prague we did not realise that we had felt a loss in our identity, specifically our culturally blended identity, when we moved to New Zealand in 2006. It was not until we began the conversation in Prague that we unravelled and recognised that we had been going through grief all this time.

Grief felt due to a loss of your identity is a different kind of pain than the more immediate and heart-breaking pain that happens when you lose a person. Grief when associated with a loss of your identity is subtle, underlying, unpredicted and can go undetected for some time. However, a loss of your identity does bring up similar emotions to grieving the loss of a person such as sadness, emptiness, crying, isolation, anger, lack of motivation, pessimism and negativity. Because I never associated grief with anything other than a loss of a person, I never registered that I was going through grief when I moved. When grief goes undetected it makes it harder to heal from because the feelings I stated above will continue to circulate inside of you with no resolve. For some people, and I am one of them, grief is a feeling almost like a wallpaper that is undoubtedly there but is not the centre of attention, it just exists in the background. You might want to strip the wallpaper and change it, but you do not have the tools or know how to change it. This is where recognising that you are going through grief is important because then you can use the right healing tools to understand and prosper through grief, and you then have a choice to change the grief wallpaper that is part of you or leave the wallpaper as it is and accept it.

What forms your identity is anything associated with who you are which includes places, people, cultures, countries, connections, traditions, rituals, senses of achievement, senses of belonging and your sense of home. I have felt grief in my identity most when I have moved and lived in different countries. It is important to state that each CBP will have their own version of how grief has come into their life. It may not necessarily be related to a physical move. This deep dive is primarily a story of the grief I felt when I moved because that was when grief was felt the most for me. As a reader, think about your own version of your identity grief story even if it is not associated to you moving. The application of the grief stages and essence of gains and losses is what will be relatable throughout any version of identity grief felt as a CBP.

With each physical move to a new place that occurred in my life I experienced some gains and some losses. Each time that I moved I had to give up things I did not initially predict I would have to give up. I lost constants in my life that I once had found comfort in that provided me with a sense of belonging and home. In my case, the moves I made were outwardly for positive reasons. Because of this initial positive reason, it allowed the grief I felt to go unnoticed and undetected for a long time.

I do want to acknowledge that although the moves that I made were for the better it is also important to point out that not everyone gets to move for the better. Sometimes people must leave a place because they are forced or required to move, for example, refugees who cannot stay in their country anymore or expats who are forced to leave the country that they have been working in. During the coronavirus pandemic there were countless redundancies across the world that forced people to leave a country they were working in and move. If someone moves because they are forced to move it can be expected that they might feel sadness, loss, emptiness or isolation. However, if someone moves and the reason for that move is to create or experience a better situation one would assume that the person would not experience any sense of grief, sadness, loss, emptiness or isolation. Despite these assumptions I experienced grief even though the move was planned and wanted. This grief soon became a reality because I lost things that were a part of my identity. I experienced changes, such as different societal norms, traditions that stopped or became less celebrated, and a day-to-day life that was slightly or even completely different. This made me feel sad, it made me cry, it made me upset, and it made me long for what I once had that I would never be able to have again exactly how it used to be. When I moved to New Zealand that was just the beginning of all the future moves I was going to have, and there was a weighted and dampening feeling I felt that I could not explain to myself or to anyone else.

I will be unravelling three stages of grief in regard to the loss felt in one's identity. These are stages I have formulated from experience. Unlike the five or sometimes seven stages associated with traditional grief, I have narrowed it down to three. I have named these stages Unaware, Loss and Acceptance. When dealing with grief due to a loss of identity, your experience can be compared to the shape of a U. Your emotions start on a high then dip down to a pit, the bottom of the U-shape, and then this is followed by a feeling that rises back up to a high. It is paramount to recognise that when going through grief there will come a time when you point back towards the sky. This deep dive is an encouragement to uncover, think about, and work through any grief you have felt when you have lost a part of who you are, your identity, so that you can heal and prosper.

The Unaware Stage

The first stage of grief when losing your identity is when you are at the top of the U and begin to decline to the bottom. You are unaware that grief is slowly creeping in. The crux of the reason of why this is the unaware stage is because the effects of losing a part of your identity is unpredictable because it is not necessarily immediate. The grief that I experienced was slow growing, it was in the background like a wallpaper. Other things were going on in my life, so I was distracted and was unaware.

When I first moved to New Zealand in 2006, I was unaware that I would be experiencing grief in losing part of my identity. There was excitement, nervousness, fear, anxiousness, discovery, motivation and a desire for change when my parents told me that we were going back home, so to speak, to New Zealand, even though I had never lived there before. When I first moved to Methven, I was excited. I was excited to be a New Zealander among all the other New Zealanders in New Zealand. I was excited to have a Kiwi home, go to a Kiwi school and do Kiwi things. I was so excited to just fit right in with other people just like me, so I assumed. For a few months everything was new. My mind and energy were consumed by all these new things. I was not focused on what I did not have anymore and what was going to become less accessible. I was unaware that with a gain, in my case of gaining a new place to live in New Zealand, that this came coupled with losses that I did not predict.

The Loss Stage

At the bottom of the shape of the U there is a lull and this is the lowest point in the grief cycle. After the first stage of being unaware it leads into loss which encompasses a variety of feelings such as not belonging, loneliness, and homesickness. I remember having feelings of being not relatable, weird, different, abnormal and foreign. These feelings are unique to each individual, yet all have a commonality in that your identity cannot purely exist the way it once had. This induces a feeling of loss of the tangible or invisible things you once had. Examples of these can include a connection to a sound, certain types of people, a country, a home, a culture, a once common place or a once celebrated tradition. You begin to now recognise that you have lost things that were always there and supported the perception of the identity that you have of yourself. This feeling of loss is grief. When you do not recognise it as grief then you can stay in the lull of the U for a long time because you do not have the tools that come with first identifying and then mending the grief that you are experiencing.

I remember an event vividly when we first moved to New Zealand. My mum, sister and I were driving back to Methven after dropping my dad off at the Christchurch Airport as he was flying to Sydney that day. I was in the front seat happily looking out the window when I turned to say something to my mum and I saw that her eyes were welling with tears. I decided not to say anything and turned back to look out the window again. I was a little bit startled at seeing my mum cry. I had only ever seen her tear up at rom coms so seeing her with tears in her eyes now made me wonder nervously what she could be crying about. There is something about parents crying that makes you unsettled as a child. To me I was the one that cried because I was the kid and my parents helped me work through my problems. To me my parents were the strongest part of the family and I did not think they had weaknesses of any kind. I was thinking about what my mum could be crying about when it came to me that my mum had left her husband at the airport to go to another country. Although my dad often left the country we were in to fly to another country as part of his job, I continued to wonder why my mum would be crying about leaving my dad at the airport when it was working out well that we now had a family home in two separate countries. My parents had planned on having two homes given our situation and as it turned out we still spent a great deal of time together as a family. Despite knowing all of this, worry started to creep in because I knew something was wrong in my mum's life but I did not know what it could be. To see the core strength of the family show weakness meant that something was seriously wrong in my eyes.

I never ended up asking my mum what she was crying about that day and because I never did I never knew until writing this book that there were so many things regarding her identity and belonging that she was going through that brought on a feeling of loss. She was also dealing with her own grief and similar to me she was not aware that what she was experiencing was a slow growing, undetected type of grief. When you are not aware then it makes it difficult to talk about and it makes it harder to work through and get over. In this way the feelings circulate unresolved inside of you for a long time.

Because I never asked Mum that day, I had no idea that she was immigrating to New Zealand. I never knew about the complications and negative flow-on effects that came from her immigration story. Not that it was a negative process but there was an emptiness felt in the defeat and isolation she had when the lawyer told her she only had three months in New Zealand before she had to leave, because she was an American. She was labelled as a visiting American. In terms of her identity, she had been involved with the New Zealand way of life ever since she met my dad and she was the one that educated my sister and I on New Zealand when we were growing up in Dubai. New Zealand had become part of her identity that included her husband and children's identity. When she was only labelled as an American by the immigration officer without a right to live in New Zealand, as technically she was only an American by citizenship, there was a sense of loss in the fact that she resonated with New Zealand and it was unrecognisable by other people. But how could other people recognise that New Zealand was a part of her identity when she sounded American and only had American citizenship?

I never knew she was going through this because it was not something she wanted to share with her two young kids at the time and more importantly she was in the stage of grief to not fully be aware of why she felt as she did. I never knew until writing this book that her experiences of the legality to live in New Zealand started the ball rolling for her to feel as though she was never fully accepted in New Zealand. It is important to say that this feeling lasted for many years but is not the result or fault of any New Zealanders that purposefully made her feel this way. The reason that she never felt fully accepted in New Zealand is because she felt she was losing her identity that she once knew and was not able to own her culturally blended identity. Part of the reason for this stems from the fact that as people continue to ask her the question *where are you from* she is continually met with "no you are not, where are you really from" responses. This is the crux of her grief with the loss of her own identity. She is a cultural blend, her own unique blend, that until we began having conversations and writing this book she never fully absorbed.

Another part of the grief that my Mum felt had to do with her losing, or feeling that she was losing, her connection with her first home in America. Since my parents made the decision to settle the family into New Zealand the option of Mum ever living in the USA again was slipping away and eventually it was completely gone. Again, this is a perfect example of with every gain comes a loss. I now realise that she felt an underlying grief as the years went on that she could never live in her country of origin ever again. She could never live near her parents or siblings again and with that came a loss of a life she had given up when choosing to settle in New Zealand. The United States was a part of her identity that she was losing touch with and at the same time she was trying to grow her identity in New Zealand. It was at this time that she was feeling, although not fully recognising, that she was losing sight of her own identity which induces a state of feeling rootless and not belonging anywhere.

When I was in high school my mum sat down with my sister and I and told us that she was giving up her American citizenship and asked us how we would feel about that. She explained the reason for this which I understood. After a few minutes I said it was fine and left the room, yet it bothered me. The more I thought about it the more upset I became. My mum had always been the American and I was an American because of her so I wondered if my American citizenship would somehow be affected, which it was not. I thought about previous conversations I had with my mum when she told me there was a rule that when I turned 18, I would only be able to have one citizenship, either my New Zealand or American citizenship. That rule has since changed yet the decision of choosing between two parts of who I am was heart-breaking. To not be an American anymore or to not be a New Zealander anymore was inconceivable to me. How could I even explain myself to others anymore? I could not help but think that if I had to choose one citizenship over the other, I would feel like a part of me, who I am as a person, had died. I wondered if my mum felt this way when choosing to renounce her American citizenship.

The years following my Mum renouncing her American citizenship resulted in things changing. Each time after that she travelled to the United States she was treated differently when going through American customs. She was always held up at the immigration desk and questioned. On top of this, she now only had a limited amount of time, three weeks, that she could spend in the USA each year. The legality of my mum's citizenship and the paper it was written on changed but what I could not understand was how that one document could take the American part of my mum's identity away from her. Regardless of having citizenship, a passport or not, America was still part of her identity. This caused a grief in her that she did not fully recognise until we began having conversations that led to writing this book. It brought up questions about how legal documentation seems to be more important in defining one's identity than what one feels on the inside. This was exactly how I felt in my connection to Dubai. I found it difficult to justify to people that I was actually from Dubai when I was not a citizen and I have no legal documentation other than the residency visa I had until I turned 19. The more I found it difficult to justify to other people that Dubai was where I was from I realised that I was now finding it hard to justify it to myself. I felt a loss of who I was and my identity because for a time I was convinced that legal documentation seemed like the only thing that mattered.

What bothered me about my mum renouncing her citizenship was that it affected my American identity emotionally. Neither my mum nor I had any idea that this would happen. Since moving to New Zealand all the American things we did started to lose momentum. The longer we spent in New Zealand the less my mum wanted to celebrate American things because she was trying to grow her identity as a New Zealander. She wanted to embrace being a New Zealander because New Zealand was the place she chose to settle, it was where she gained citizenship, it was part of her future and it had always felt like her home since the day she was married more than 30 years ago. Thanksgiving, Christmas and the Fourth of July were always big events in our neighbourhood in Dubai. It was my mum that organised these. It was a way to share our culture with our friends. She invited everyone over to our house and we always had family dinner parties where all nationalities were involved. To her it did not matter that people were not American and they did not care either. In Dubai it was common to celebrate each other's traditions and culture. This was similar to International Day at my primary school where we celebrated our own cultures and took part and celebrated cultures that were not ours. These big festive American events that involved everyone and that I looked forward to stopped when we came to New Zealand. When I was young it made me upset that my mum did not seem to care about them as much. These festivities and traditions were a big part of my American identity. Upon arriving in New Zealand, without expecting it or pre-dicting it, the American part of my identity began to wither away. My mum was the centre of my American identity and is the reason I am American so to see her give that up made me miss what I once had. I learned later during our conversations after our trip to Prague that my mum did not feel as comfortable celebrating these traditions in New Zealand outwardly as she did in Dubai. It seemed that the main cele-brations to her in New Zealand would be those that were connected to New Zealand. She began to celebrate those American traditions in her own way. Despite the reasons that she stopped celebrating American things, I realised that I was in fact grieving for my past which I could not get back. I was not aware that I was going through grief. Because I did not recognise this grief it went undetected for years and remained unresolved.

Going back to when I first arrived in New Zealand and after the initial period of excitement wore off, I came to the realisation that I was beginning to resent New Zealand because I was losing touch with America. The dilemma with being a dual citizen is that you are not always in a position where you can live in both places. One place has to be chosen primarily over the other. When my family chose to settle in New Zealand, I lost something I did not want to lose and the only thing I had to blame was moving to New Zealand. There was this tug and pull of national identities I was going through. I had a resentment towards New Zealand because I felt it took away the American part of my identity. Yet, I also wanted to embrace and be recognised as a New Zealander. The result of this tugging from opposite directions at my identity was that I felt as if I was not from either place. I felt that I could never be just me as I was in parts that felt scattered. This made me feel that somehow I was not fully whole. I experienced deep feelings of rootlessness, homesickness, missing things I once had and also feeling as if I was not a true New Zealander. These feelings all culminated into a grief that I did not recognise and therefore could not work through.

After my mum and I had many conversations regarding these issues after our trip to Prague, I began to realise some things. One thing was that daily life in New Zealand was very different from life in Dubai. At first it was exciting and new but after a while it started to feel uncomfortable because it was not what I was used to. When things change around us our view of our identity is changed too. This is referred to as our sensory identity which is defined as identity based on the manner in which we relate to external stimuli received through our senses which form internal perceptions of ourselves in relation to others. One example is when I would go to sleep in New Zealand it was quiet with only a few crickets chirping in the background. I remember feeling strange and uncomfortable because it was so eerily quiet. I was accustomed to hearing the cars all night long on the Sheikh Zayed Road by my house in Dubai. The constant hum of cars passing was like white noise to me and it always put me to sleep. I was also accustomed to hearing the call to prayer throughout the day in Dubai from the mosques. I most noticeably enjoyed hearing the comforting sounds of the call to prayer when I would go to sleep and wake up. Even though I am not Muslim I had an attachment to living in a country that em-braced the Muslim traditions because I identified those sounds with comfort and home. When I moved to New Zealand, I never heard the call to prayer at night or in the morning (or throughout the day for that matter) and life felt out of place. I felt this growing pain because I was always missing things that I identified with, and I felt that I had lost part of myself.

I eventually have come to realise that when I was in Dubai it was there that all the three parts of my identity coexisted. I was an American New Zealander living in Dubai which to me was and will always be my first home and where I feel that I am from. During the time that my dad continued to work in Dubai I knew that I always had the connection to at least go back and be in that space where I feel complete. However, as I have previously mentioned, things changed dramatically when Covid took its effect on the world. I know that many family's lives were affected by the results of the pandemic of 2020 that continues even as we finish this book in 2022. I know that many children will be like me, they will have left places that they called home to go to another place that they are told is their home. To me nothing can replace my home in Dubai. Home is more than just a building it is a feeling. It took a while for the reality to sink in that I had lost my home in Dubai and that I will never be able to go back there the way I always used to. I can always travel to Dubai and stay in a hotel but it will never be the same as taking the familiar road back to my house from the airport. It is an incredibly sad feeling and was out of my control so, therefore, the grief continued to linger. I would look at old photos of my family in Dubai and cry because I missed it so much and the weight of the feeling came on heavy because those reminiscing moments always ended with the sadness that life will never be the same. I would watch as my friends in New Zealand would go back to their hometowns throughout the country after the national Covid lockdown was lifted but I could not. This was something that still sets me apart from other New Zealanders, despite being a New Zealander myself, even after fifteen years of permanently living there. My home of over twenty years in Dubai is gone forever and that filled my world with a loss that was difficult to find a solution to as nothing else compared to it and it could not be replaced by anything in New Zealand. My identity is so connected to Dubai and I lost that connection, like someone cut off the string that attached me to where I find my identity. Things in life change all the time and they come coupled with gains and losses, yet the losses can saturate the gains. The losses can become the only thing you focus on which takes the joy away from the gains. With this it also becomes difficult to adjust your identity with new changes as instead it remains stagnant and unwilling to change with new periods of life. This is what happens when the grief goes unresolved.

Having a loss in your identity is hurtful, sad, and can fill your world with a constant missing of something that you once had. It was not until my mum and I had that conversation under the vines in Prague that I told my mum about the time I saw her crying in the car after we dropped my dad off at the airport in 2006. It was then that the long overdue conversation began about the grief felt for each of us when moving to New Zealand. Even among families, perceptions and experiences are different and it cannot be assumed that you know how the other people are feeling because usually, in this type of identity grief, we do not talk about it because we do not know how to talk about it. We just feel the effects of it and cannot associate it with grief to apply the right tools to heal and prosper.

The Acceptance Stage

In this final stage, the acceptance stage, you start to rise up from the bottom of the U and eventually reach the top again. There are two considerations to this that will help you overcome the grief you have felt and patch together your identity with a new perception of loss and more importantly the gains that come with it, however big or small they are. Although it may seem cliche to say this, think about the good instead of the bad. The acceptance stage is like a workout, you have to be committed to it to gain results even though it can be difficult. The results do not always appear immediately but over time you will see a change if you stick to reframing your mind about what you have lost. I can give advice and perceptions but the acceptance stage is about your decision to not allow the things you have lost be a burden on your identity any longer.

The first consideration is the internal quest to fill the emptiness you have felt in your identity through the stage of loss. I mentioned in the loss stage, referring to my house in Dubai, that I do not think I will ever be able to find a replacement for it. Sometimes it is possible to find replacements and sometimes it is not. Even if you can find a re-placement it sometimes just 'isn't quite the same' so there can still be an emptiness felt. You can either fill the holes in your identity with getting what you had back into your life, or you can change your mindset to fill the holes with love for what you once had. In the case where it is not possible to have what you once had back in your life, you need to have a talk with yourself and tell yourself that you are a walking embodiment of all the experiences, connections, relationships, cultures and/or countries that make up your identity. You need to understand and realise that there are no holes in your identity, you have just let triggers and changes in life make you feel as if you are not whole. The quest to fill the holes is the quest to realise that things may be gone physically but emotionally they are always there because they are circulating in your mind and they are part of who you are as a person. It helps for me to think about my memories of what I once had because I am reminded that my past is still present in my memories. This makes me feel as if I am not losing touch with what I once had. I still replace and recreate certain things in my life like American traditions (even if it is not with other Americans). I have decorations in my room in New Zealand that remind me of America and Dubai. To me it provides the essence of home in my present life that I have accepted as a part of my new life. It is important to accept that things do not always stay the same.

The second consideration is to have a new relationship with how you view changes, losses and gains. Accept that change is inevitable. Accept that just because things change around you that your identity does not change with it. Accept that change is a natural occurrence and ride the wave instead of anchoring where you will constantly be bounced around by the tide and will not feel at peace. Specific to my experience with grief, I mentioned in the loss stage that I thought legal documentation was the only thing that mattered and the validity of my identity was placed so dependently on that fact, especially when it came to feeling as if I am from Dubai. When I turned 19, I lost my residency visa to the UAE. I felt that since I did not have heritage from Dubai, a passport or residency visa, or a home in Dubai then that made it less valid for me to tell people I am from Dubai. After time, and that is the resounding thing with grief is that it takes time, I accepted that legal documentation does not matter if I choose to not let it matter to me. I am still from Dubai and I have come to a mindset that I accept when people disagree with me because they have never lived my life. They could never understand the wholesome connection I have with Dubai and how my identity is so importantly centred there. It is the same with my mum renouncing her American citizenship, a piece of paper may have been lost but her identity with the USA is still valid because it is a part of who she is.

The same thing applies in the first as it does in the second consideration. You need to take the importance out of the physical and rely on the emotional connections so that your identity can feel alive in any new change of your life. I have accepted the fact that change is an inevitable part of life and with change comes gains and losses. In this way I have freed myself from the anchor that has previously put me in unsettled waters as I am now able to ride the waves comfortably without an anchor. I encourage you to be at peace with that fact of life and find ways to work around it in a creative way to allow your true identity to be alive. You will achieve this by changing your mindset.

One of the best ways that I have found to start changing my mindset is to start by being grateful and adopting a gratitude mindset. Gratefulness is a peaceful way to transition to the acceptance stage and it is the mental space you need to rest in. The best way I can describe how to deal with losses and gains is something I learnt through meditation. The metaphor given was that in your life you can have clouds fill your sky. It can rain, hail, thunder and leave you in a dark space which sometimes leads you to thinking that it will never end. This kind of atmosphere can make you feel miserable and sad. The metaphor continues to describe that if you ever look at the clouds they move constantly so the storm will never stay but the most important recognition is that the sun is always, always shining above the clouds. There will never not be a time when the sun is not shining or even the moon is not twinkling for that matter because that is not the way our atmosphere works. Compare your identity to the always shining sun, losses in life to the clouds and gains to the silver lining in the clouds. The ultimate thing to realise that will bring you peace and acceptance is that clouds come and go and even if they are above you for a long time, the sun and hence your identity is still shining above it so your identity is never truly lost, only hidden.

To conclude with this chapter on grief, I encourage you to start having conversations with yourself or with other people who have gone through a similar thing. Reframe your mindset so that identity does not have to be dependent on the physical but on the emotion of how you connect to what you have lost and the gains that come with it. It is important that you are in the driver's seat of how you perceive yourself internally and how you define yourself to other people. Again, gratitude is one of the highest mental healing powers that you can choose to adopt. It will give you the willpower to rise up from the lull of the U and shine always as you.

Lorraine's Deep Dive of

GRIEF

IN MY CONVERSATIONS that I have had with other people who identify with being culturally blended, many have a story of grief. It is important to understand that grief does not always hit like a lightning strike. To feel grief, one does not wake up one morning and say, "I'm grieving". Of course, you do if the grief is caused by something like the sudden death of a loved one. However, the grief that Ashley and I had conversations about refer to the grief that grows slowly like mould, undetected for a long time, hardly noticeable, often unexplainable as to its mere existence, but always unwanted. As I look back on the timeline beginning when I first left the United States in 1987 until now, I can recognise the slow increments of grief that were forming, going undetected yet scarring my inner identity.

The first example of a slow growing, hardly detectable but lingering type of grief that I will share with you would seem insignificant to many people. In fact, it is in writing this book that I find it is the first time I am sharing the full story with anyone. When Ashley was born, I remember wrestling with this choice of what would my daughter call me, Mom as is used in America or Mum which is used in New Zealand. I can remember the emotional turmoil I had, just prior to Ashley learning how to talk, when I was forced to make the final decision, Mom or Mum. When I tried to explain this dilemma to others at the time it was found comical, and in a way, I suppose it was. As it happened in Dubai, most of my daughters' friends used the word mum.

When Ashley was born, Wayne and I had a long-term plan that we would eventually leave Dubai and move to New Zealand. It made more sense to me to have my daughters call me Mum. This is an example of trying to fit in instead of standing out. I have now been called Mum for more than 20 years, yet I cannot explain why but I still feel a sad twang when I remember the preconceived idea of who I would be as a mother and what I would be called. The term mom is very American, it always will be, and it personally holds a special place of endearment in my heart. I never refer to my mom as mum. My parents always told me stories about their mom.

I wrestled, trying to discover, this inner sadness that was spawned by the Mom vs Mum dilemma. With deep reflection I realised that what bothered me is that I had to choose. The reality is that a choice brings an inevitable loss. A choice is just that, a welcoming of one gain and the loss of its opposite. The inevitable loss that comes with choice is the loss that is connected to grief and is something that Culturally Blended People experience. On a different perspective of the same issue the reality that I became a mum and not a mom made it feel like my Americanness was breaking and slowly floating away. In Dubai I made it a top priority to keep American traditions alive so that I could have a sense of my homeland outside of my homeland. I always imagined that I would be a mom one day and I wondered what kind of mom I would be. To then not become a mom but a mum, although exactly the same thing, I lost this sense of an American attachment to my identity as a mother and with that to my identity as a whole.

The scorpion's tail that exists with choice is that in choosing one you lose the other. The issue is when a choice has to be made concerning your own identity, you may face the reality that you are choosing between parts of you which will inevitably spiral into an emptiness. When one feels this emptiness, one experiences loss and even in the smallest of circumstances this can lead to a sense of grief. Grief is something to acknowledge and to work through and then to discover a new place of acceptance.

Ashley referred to the choice that she would have had to make when she turned 18, to choose either her New Zealand citizenship or her American citizenship if the law had not changed. This rule has, however, changed and she never had to make the choice. However, before this change happened, the struggle to make the impending choice was real and difficult. Ashley never had to choose to give up her American citizenship or her New Zealand citizenship. Many people have had to make this choice and it is a choice that they never wanted to make. How does one choose to lose half of their identity because of a law?

There are instances in life where one cannot choose between two different things. Let me offer this example as a further way to explain this concept. This example is not directly related to being a cultural blend but shares the reality people face when choosing is not an option. I remember when Ashley's sister was born. Many of my friends at the time were mothers like myself and most had only one child. One of my friends asked me, honestly wanting to know, "How can you love two children when all the love you have you have given to the first one? Where do you get extra love for the second one or do you split the love that you have?" I pondered what she said at the time when we welcomed a new baby sister for Ashley into the family. How was I able to love one child and then when the second child was born, not love the first one any less, as if I had to share the love, but love the second child equally as much? How did it happen? It happened because I never had to make a choice of how much love I would give the first child and save the rest for the second child. My answer to my friend was a profound moment in my life, one of those moments that happens as a parent. I explained to my friend, "When you have only one child you can only imagine loving that one child and cannot imagine how your love will be shared when another comes along. Yet, I can promise you, when the second child is born a whole new bundle of love to give seems to just instantly arrive with the new child. I cannot explain it, but you do not have to make a choice. There is enough love for both, and that love given is unique to each." This is the same concept that can be applied to a Culturally Blended Person who cannot imagine not loving and being connected to each part of who they are. The reason that this causes grief is that when someone asks a CBP *where are you from* there is an expectation that one geographic place will be given. A CBP cannot love one part of themselves and give the other part up. When they are asked the question *where are you from* they want to give the answer that incorporates all parts of them. This can include multiple geographic places. It is common when a person answers with all the places that they find their own identity that they are met with a reply such as, "No, where are you really from?" or "Which part are you?" or "But you sound like, or you look like you are from…" When met with such a reply a CBP is met with a challenge to their personal identity and a form of grief begins to be felt.

As this chapter on grief comes to a close, it is important to reiterate how grief works and what can be discovered as one moves through it. Ashley shared the stages that she has identified in her grief process. Grief often starts undetected and can go unnoticed for some time. Once the awareness of a loss is discovered it is normal to first be in denial, to show frustration, and to enter into stages of depression. Ashley and I have worked together through our individual grief by engaging in conversations with each other. We have discovered the losses we have experienced, shared our feelings and thoughts which led us on a pathway to the final stage of grief, the moment of acceptance. It is important to remember that grief is as individual as a person's fingerprint. Each person will move through the stages of grief in their own way and in their own time.

This deep dive is an encouragement to dive into your own unresolved grief in the course of you claiming your identity on your terms. Your identity is unique to you and is part of the story that you write for yourself based on your life and your experiences.

7

DEFINING HOME

SATURDAY MORNING IN PRAGUE
The American in New Town

Ashley

IT WAS A crisp Saturday morning and we once again headed out the fancy red door, this time towards New Town where we had not yet been to explore. As we approached the Charles Bridge we stopped to read the plaque nailed to the medieval stone archway. The Charles Bridge began construction in 1357 and was finished at the beginning of the fifteenth century. Back in those days, this bridge was the only way to cross the Vltava River until about 1841. It was an important connection between the various boroughs of Prague and served as the pathway of coming to and from home for the people of Prague. Stoic statues of notable saints and figures bordered the bridge and the dark smoky sculptures rose above the pedestrians and appeared almost alive in a ghostlike way.

Today there was a lively market sprawled out along the bridge. We decided to take a detour to walk across the bridge and back. The crowd was an assortment of bustling locals whizzing through the slow-paced tourists who were marvelling at the features of the bridge and the wares for sale in the stalls. Sellers were lined up on either side of the bridge with their tables full of handmade items which included everything from jewellery and fashion to pottery and paintings. Intrigued by the market festivities, we slowed our pace to take in all that the morning had to offer.

As we walked across the bridge, my mum spent time admiring the items in detail on the tables and stands while I spent time admiring the statues along the balustrade more closely. As we made our way slowly between the tables, my mum met one friendly Italian women selling jewellery and she ended up having a fairly long conversation with her that I overheard. She learnt that she was originally from Florence and married a man from Prague. My mum shared with her how she too had married a man from another country and immigrated into his country. After my mum moved on from that table, she said to me how special it is to meet people in various corners of the world who have experienced a similar life to hers. They both were part of a marriage that was fused together by different cultures, and both made a new home in their husband's country.

Once we had walked up and down the bridge we headed off towards New Town. We found this cool, modern cafe with long windows nestled in an ancient and smoky building and headed through the glossy door. The first thing that caught my eye when we entered was the extravagant display of different coffee plungers showcased on shelves and nooks around the room. This cafe had a minimalistic, bold, science lab vibe on the inside that was a nice contrast from the ancient exteriors. The styles were from different eras, but they blended together in the most fabulous way. The smells from the kitchen wafted under my nose and my eyes became transfixed on the food cabinet. Each food item was free of something. Free of gluten, free of diary or free of GMO. This was just our kind of place. After ordering we noticed a free spot on a bar table that looked out the long windows. We perched ourselves on the red stools and waited patiently for our coffee and treats to arrive. We engaged in light conversation about the sights of the day so far.

Along the bar from us was a man reading quietly. After a short time, he turned to us and in an American accent said, "I don't often hear English being spoken around here, where are you two from?" A lively conversation began as my mum and I shared our story and then he shared his story about where he was from. We learned that he was born and raised in Argentina as his parents worked there. When he was nine years old his family moved to Philadelphia in Pennsylvania as they were Americans by citizenship. He said he had been living there ever since but last year he had become increasingly interested in his heritage which he had traced back to Prague. He then decided he wanted to move and live around Europe for a while, discovering his family and also discovering more of the world. He made a comment that as soon as he got to Prague, he felt a connection and was looking for ways to be able to make this place home for a while like his ancestors.

We conversed back and forth about what it was like growing up in Argentina, the UAE, New Zealand and the USA. We talked about the various cultures we experienced, the travelling that we did, and how we each identified as a Culturally Blended Person. It was fascinating to meet someone who could relate to us in this city where we felt quite different from those around us. He was the kind of person we had been talking about existing in this world all along. In this cool, modern cafe we had an interesting and memorable conversation about our lives and where we call home with another Culturally Blended Person.

Ashley's Deep Dive of

DEFINING HOME

HOW DO YOU actually define home? What is required for a place to be considered a home? What is typically thought of when you think of a home? Is it a house, town, city or country? No, it is more than that. Home is actually a multifaceted word that you probably have never considered it to be, especially in a culturally blended way of life perspective. Home is comfort and a sense of belonging. It is somewhere that you feel rooted but at the same time it is a state of mind, not limited to a physical house, town, city or country. It can be more than that too. Your definition of home can change over time as you experience different things. Your concept of home can evolve as your comforts and sense of belonging become redefined by different seasons in your life.

Defining home is similar to how to define the word *from* in the context of the question *where are you from*. Where does *from* actually begin? Does it begin at birth? If that is the case, then my sister should be able to say she is from Dubai without question since she was born there. Yet if she does say she is from Dubai then people say, "No. Where are you really from?" This is because she does not look and sound like someone that is stereotypically from Dubai. Does where you are from rely on your first citizenship? If that is the case, then my mum is only from the USA. Yet how does that work when she renounced her American citizenship and is legally only a New Zealand citizen? Does *where are you from* begin at current citizenship? If that is the case, then my mum should be able to say she is a New Zealander without question, but she frequently receives follow-up questions about where she is really from because she does not sound like a New Zealander due to her lingering American twang. But how relevant is an accent? So, does *where are you from* begin at genetic heritage? How far back in your lineage must you go to establish an accepted answer to the question *where are you from*? Hypothetically, if someone was to disagree with me being from New Zealand or America would I say I am from Poland, France, or Scotland? Each of these places are more than seven generations ago for me. More importantly, I have no personal connection with these places that are part of my genetic makeup. Therefore, by other people defining you by your genetic heritage, no matter how far back it goes and whether or not you identify with that place, it completely takes away the point of the question *where are you from* and changes it to where are your ancestors from. With the contradictions that exist of the different meanings of the word from in the question *where are you from*, how is it possible to only use one of them to be the accurate meaning? It is in the same way that the meaning of home is subjective because it depends on what you have experienced in life in terms of where you have felt a homely connection, what you find comfort in, what you have experienced and where you feel that you belong. If you are searching for a simple solution on how to define home for yourself then in this chapter you will not find it because home has many meanings and it will mean something different to everyone. This chapter will help you discover how to define home in your own original culturally blended way of life.

For a Culturally Blended Person, it can feel like a hopeless task to try to define home because usually you do not fit the traditional mould of having one physical home that you connect with as a person. You may feel as if there are multiple barriers getting in the way of you truly defining home for yourself. Attempting to define home when you have lived a life that is outside the ordinary, extraordinary for that matter, but nevertheless quite different to others can be a task that you do not know how to begin. It is a task that can cause you grief, make you question your identity, make you feel as if you do not belong anywhere, make you feel as if you are missing out and make you feel as if your life is weird. Having a home is instinctual for humans. Each of us wants to find somewhere comfortable to nest and this chapter will help you find the twigs to do so.

There are many different situations that people are in that make trying to define home something that is not simple but has many layers to it. You might define home as a country, one where you have citizenship or not. Even though you have citizenship to a country you might be in a situation where you can no longer go back to that country. You might define home as a physical house. In this case you might be in a situation where you can no longer go back to that house as was the case with my house in Dubai. You might be like myself and not have the correct legal documentation to the place you call home. You might define home as a group of people that you relate to. In this case you might feel that homely feeling when you are among other Culturally Blended People that give you a sense of belonging somewhere. You might define home as a culture that is part of a country. You might consider home more than one physical place and is a combination of two or more places. These examples showcase how home can take a different form and therefore its definition is subjective depending on what one experiences in their life. It also demonstrates issues that can exist that create turbulence for you in clarifying exactly how to define home.

It is important to realise as a CBP that home can be defined by the traditional form of a house, town or country but it can also transcend the idea that it is a physical place because comfort and a sense of belonging can be found in so many different things. Home does not always have to be location based, it can be made up of elements such as memories, traditions, routines, foods, experiences, landscapes, smells, architecture, weather, connections, people and community to say the least. The link between all of these things, the physical and invisible, is that there is comfort and belonging felt which gives you that sensation of home. The sensation that feels like home can also be felt anywhere. Have you ever been in a hotel room, Airbnb, family member's house, friend's house or any location and something about it feels like home? It is not your physical home or hometown but something about it has a homely feel. This happens because home is a state of mind and the things that remind you of home can be found in different corners of the world. When this happens, you may find that as you move in life you can settle in a new place easily because something about it feels like home. You possibly even sought out this place due to the fact that it reminds you of the home or parts of home you had in a different place in time. This leads into the next reality of home that it is also a place in time. It is a natural human instinct to adapt to one's surroundings and when you do this you begin to grow new roots and resonate with elements of your new stage in life. When this occurs, you will begin to grow new comforts, belonging and with that begin to alter your definition of home to assimilate this new phase of life. In an opposite way, you may move to a new place that you are unable to integrate due to a new place feeling so foreign or you do not want to integrate the new parts of your life into what you consider as home. This can be caused by a reaction to a subconscious rejection that you are having to a new place that does not initially feel like home. This will become a barrier to fully establishing a feeling of comfort and belonging to a new place. When this occurs the perception of home needs to be altered so that the idea of home is made up of elements that are both physical and invisible. To achieve this, you can recreate the old elements of life and blend it into your new phase of life which is the natural process of redefining home. If you are a person struggling to define home, first think about what elements in your life give you comfort, a sense of belonging and be sure to include both physical and invisible attributes.

I will give four examples of how I define home differently in Dubai, USA, Canada and New Zealand. Each are very different in how they feel like home to me, yet they all fall under the same umbrella of the word home. It reiterates the point that home is a multifaceted word that is completely original and subjective to each person, especially CBPs who have lived a life outside the traditional. I have mentioned before that you need to see the mould of you and how you define home as malleable and can evolve as you experience new seasons in your life.

Dubai

In April of 2018 I was at the Pearsons International Airport in Toronto, Canada. I had just spent six months in Whistler during the winter season and was going home to Dubai for two weeks during the break between the winter and summer seasons. I walked up to the Emirates check-in desk and handed my ticket and passport over to the lady at the counter. After a lot of typing, clicking and scrolling she peered around her screen and asked, "Do you have a return ticket?" I replied, "No." She said, "You need a return ticket to go to Dubai as you do not have a residency visa or citizenship and are a tourist. I cannot let you board the plane because when you arrive in Dubai, they might not let you clear customs." I was startled at hearing this as I had never had to deal with this before. I have mentioned before, that up until I turned 19, I was issued with a residency visa to Dubai so that I could live there. I was 21 on that day and although I knew I did not have a residency visa, I never thought that I needed a return ticket upon entry into Dubai and I guess it slipped my parents' minds as well. I have travelled to Dubai after I turned 19 but I must have always had a return ticket when I checked in, so this requirement never came up. I replied, "My dad, Wayne Taylor, is a captain with Emirates Airlines and he was going to book me a flight to Seattle in about two weeks depending on the loads as I will be using a standby ticket." She thought then said, "Give me a moment," and called someone on the phone.

I stood off to the side and felt a weight in my stomach, getting heavier as the time ticked by. My mind was a scramble of thoughts and questions. I messaged my parents hoping they would be awake and told them the situation. My mum replied and said that Dad was flying at the moment and she did not have his log in to book a return flight for me. She then started going through options of what I could do until he landed and could sort it out. I was in a bit of a panic because I could not believe that I could be turned down for a flight to Dubai. Can you imagine what it is like to be told you cannot go home? I experienced panic with the confronting realisation that I was being told that I can no longer go home to Dubai like I used to. It was as if Dubai was being detached from me because I did not have the correct documentation. For me, Dubai was all I had in terms of a physical home and the stark realisation that I was only a tourist in the place I felt that I belonged was soul crushing to my identity.

The lady returned to her desk and waved me over. "My supervisor has said it is okay to let you on from our end as you are identified as staff through your dad. Be aware there is no guarantee they will let you through customs in Dubai due to you being a tourist and customs may not accept the staff relation through Emirates." I said my thanks and packed away my passport and ticket, my golden ticket, that she handed to me. As I turned to leave, she quickly added in, "Be advised that tourists are issued a 30-day visiting visa upon arrival." Never before had I thought there would be this 30-day restriction in my hometown and there was a deep sense of grief in that reality. What I thought was going to be a routine check-in, one I have done numerous times in the past, had become a moment where I was being forced, against my wishes, to redefine home.

When I stepped out of the plane that had landed in Dubai and walked onto the bridge the familiar heat engulfed me like a sauna. I closed my eyes briefly enjoying that feeling of being home. I proceeded to go through customs without a problem and walked through the sliding glass doors to meet my mum. Within 24 hours of me arriving in Dubai, my sister was returning from New Zealand and my dad was returning from Thailand. I was looking forward to all of us being together again as a family. I did not know at the time that that would be the last time we would ever be all together as a family in our house in Dubai. I went back to Dubai in August later that year after I completed my air traffic control interview in New Zealand and was waiting for the results. I did not know that this trip to Dubai would be the last time I would be in that house, sleep in my room, go to my favourite restaurants, go to the Jumeriah Beach Hotel pools and go to the malls. I did not know it would be the last time I would feel the way the heat engulfs me, hear the call to prayer, see and experience the sights I had always loved. Like I said in the chapter on grief, my physical home was gone in the blink of an eye when the Covid lockdowns happened, and it was not my choice.

I went from being a resident to being a tourist. I am not a citizen and I have no genetic heritage to the UAE. For all intents and purposes, I am not someone who can call that place home on paper, yet I still do. I have had to redefine my sense of home with Dubai several times. Over a period of introspection of how I process home it has turned into a place without a foundation. It is as if it is a floating visual following me that is not reliant on or affected by documentation, restrictions and borders defined by others. As a CBP, the fundamental reality that exists is that you have the ability to manifest home on your own terms. My home is a state of mind now, it is something I replicate in my room in New Zealand with multiple trinkets I have gathered during my time from when I was a child to a young adult that remind me of Dubai. When I talk to people on the topic of home, I firstly say Dubai is my hometown and it is where I grew up. I do not let another person's view affect my view of my definition of home. In conversation with people I still say, "Back home in Dubai," whenever I recall a memory from Dubai. Sometimes I still miss it and I get emotional but that is natural when you lose something. In these moments of sadness, you have to remember the gains and memories because this is the circle of life as a CBP. Dubai is still my home. It is still where I am from regardless of legalities because I have made that decision. I own it.

The United States of America

After my two-week holiday in Dubai, I was back at the airport checking into my flight to Seattle. I was smiling from ear to ear as I had not been back to the USA for eight years. I handed over my freshly issued American passport, something I had not gotten reissued for years. After a lot of typing I was handed my ticket to Seattle. While I routinely headed through customs and walked to my gate, I had a flashback of when I travelled to Vancouver from Whistler two months prior to get my American passport reissued. Two of my friends had joined me on that day and we made a fun day trip out of it. We walked around Vancouver, went to this outrageously delicious restaurant and ate ice cream while listening to live music at a market. My appointment at the American Embassy would not take too long so my friends waited for me at a Starbucks just down the road. As I left them, I started my nervous walk towards the American flag. It was not a bad type of nervous but more of a nervous excitement because I had never gotten my American passport renewed without my parents before. This was the first time I had to do all the paperwork by myself. This process filled me with so much pride to know that legally my American identity was fully recognised. A feeling of belonging and home resurfaced to a place I had been losing touch with since moving to New Zealand. I am incredibly fortunate to have had positive and enriching experiences in the USA surrounded by family and close family friends that influenced my identity, character and perceptions. I was overcome with validation and joy as I entered the line that said American Citizens upon walking through security at the American Embassy. I went up the elevator and was taken to a booth where my appointment took place. I handed over my documents, one of them being my New Zealand passport as a form of identification. The man on the other side of the desk was very friendly. He gathered all my paperwork and took it away to process. When he came back, he handed everything over and gave me directions to where I needed to go next. He then said in the most friendly American accent, "I love your New Zealand passport, the design is the coolest of them all." There was something so incredibly touching about those words, that even though I was in the American Embassy, my New Zealand identity was being recognised and my passport, a design I share with approximately five million people, was complimented. As CBPs we take moments like these and cherish them because it means so much to have our culturally blended identity recognised in a positive way. A couple of weeks passed when I received an email saying that my passport had been sent. Each day I attentively checked our mailbox at the Whistler staff accommodation. One morning I routinely headed out of my flat to our mailbox hoping today was the day. It was a stunning day, cold but with a warm touch and the snow drifts were glistening a crystal white in the sun. I unlocked the mailbox and inside was a large envelope with my name on it. I rushed back to my flat, sat on my bed and gently opened it. I took out my crisp new passport and flicked to where my picture was. When I read Ashley Taylor with the United States of America at the top of the page I burst into tears. This sense of belonging to America wrapped me up in its comforting, homely blanket. There was something about this moment that made my identity feel whole again. For some reason, having both of my passports current is a connection my identity relies on because it means the doors are open to each country.

As CBPs, documentation both is and is not important in our identity and sense of home depending on the circumstance. I have never lived in the USA, I have never had a home there, I do not have a hometown there. Other than my family and close family friends, I do not have a group of friends there. For me, having my American passport is something I have chosen as one of the fundamental ways in which I connect to the USA. If you have ever lost a citizenship, gained a citizenship or have multiple citizenships then you may be able to relate to just how precious a passport is. My definition of home with the USA is primarily rooted in my legality, as well as, in the connections I have personally made to the environment, people, traditions, sounds, foods, smells and so much more that were part of the times I spent there when I was younger. It might seem confusing to other people, how a place can feel like home when you have never lived there, yet as a CBP I have made it possible because that is the life I have been issued and choose to acknowledge and own. I have collected different keepsakes that connect me with how the USA fits into my perception of home. I celebrate traditions, I make American foods and I display trinkets I have collected from America in my room that offers a visual way for home in America to be around me wherever I am. As in my definition of home in regard to Dubai, there is no foundation, it is purely a state of mind. The difference with the feelings I have of home in connection with the USA is that I have citizenship to this country that I cherish and grasp on to. In saying that if there ever comes a day when I choose to renounce my American citizenship, or New Zealand citizenship for that matter, I know I will have to redefine how I view home in my new era of life. I will not gain or lose a sense of home based on documentation. Life changes and things change but if you blend state of mind with place in time then you can achieve a feeling of home in your own creative way that is outside the traditional mould of home. This is an important message for CBPs trying to define home.

After my 14-hour flight from Dubai to Seattle I was once again going through customs. I handed my American passport over to the officer and he asked me some questions. "Why were you in Dubai?" I replied, "I went home to see my parents during my two-week holiday from Canada. I am on a working holiday visa in Canada as I am currently employed in Whistler." I further explained quickly that I grew up in Dubai because my dad is a pilot for Emirates. I also mentioned that I have lived in New Zealand just to cover that fact if he asked me about my accent. The officer asked, "So is New Zealand where you are from?" I replied, "Yes, actually Dubai is my home, but I am a New Zealand citizen as well and I've lived there since I was nine." He handed my passport back and then said, to the American New Zealander who grew up in Dubai standing in front of him, "Welcome home." Maybe that is something that the customs officers always say to Americans but those words I still cherish so much to this day. Despite the fact that from our conversation where I gave a brief overview of my life it was obvious I had never lived in America, he still welcomed me home.

I have defined home in America through the comforts I have grown there and the belonging to the country as a whole. This reiterates a point I made above that you can define home as a country as a whole without a specific town, city, or state within to validate it.

Canada

Intuition is a powerful feeling and one that can push you in directions in life that possibly do not seem logical but just feel right. Ever since I was young, I had this fascination with Canada for some reason and Whistler in particular. My sister and I learnt to ski at a young age in Keystone, Colorado. My ski instructor that I had in Keystone first told me about the ski resort in Whistler. I remember always asking my dad about what Canada was like when he came back from his trips to Toronto. I have this vivid memory of when I was 15 searching on the internet for information about Whistler Blackcomb Ski Resort. I was ferociously trying to discover the pathway I needed to take to land a job there. That was when I was 15 years old and that desire faded away in the back of my mind for a few years but resurfaced one year on New Year's Eve when I was by myself in my apartment in Wellington because I had to work the next day. I heard people shooting fireworks right outside my window. I closed my window to block out the noise and noticed how much hotter it got in my room because it was summer. That is when I stared at the ceiling and said to myself, I am not going to be celebrating the Christmas New Year period in summer this time next year. I was determined that in one year I would be in a cold climate. Even though I grew up in Dubai, which is assumed to be unimaginably hot, it still gets cold for winter. When I was young, my family regularly went to the United States to spend Christmas with my grandparents and auntie in Monument, Colorado where the snow would blanket the countryside and nights were spent cozied up next to the fire watching the lights of the Christmas tree twinkling in the corner. Christmas has always been in winter for me and even though I have spent several Christmas seasons in New Zealand during summer it just does not feel right. Christmas in winter has a homely feeling and I wanted to experience it again. The next morning, New Year's Day, I revisited the Whistler Blackcomb website and from there I found my pathway to Canada.

Ten months later I was on a bus enroute to Whistler. As soon as the bus drove past the wooden sign that said Whistler Village, I felt instantly at home. I had an immediate connection with Canada the second I saw the pine trees and snow because it reminded me exactly of Colorado. During my time in Colorado as a kid I developed a comfort with the landscape and I felt at home in the snowy mountains because I had a positive experience there. There were many similar things in Whistler that reminded me of the USA and in those things I found a feels like home sensation. The log cabin style of the buildings, the lakes, the pine trees, the snow, and the food were just some of those things that made me feel like I was home. I also had a homely connection to the working holiday community there because it was made up of multiple nationalities which is similar to the comfort I found in the expat community in Dubai. We were all from somewhere else and all experiencing a new country eager to grasp every experience possible and have a good time so it was easy to relate to each other. There is a comfort found in being in a group of people and growing a connection with people that are similar to you. These connections help to create that homely feeling. This reiterates a point I made before relating to the physical and invisible elements of home. In my case physical was the landscape and invisible was the friendships I made among the working holiday community. Each element made me feel at home in Canada and without realising it I was defining a different version of home in Canada compared to the definitions of home I have to other places. This is the very reason that a country I had never been to before, Canada, immediately made me feel at home. Towards the end of my

10-month working holiday in Canada I was sure that I had found my place in the world that would become my physical home too. However, my life was to take a different pathway.

I did leave Canada and did close the door to that discovery of life because I was accepted into air traffic control training and moved back to New Zealand. I blamed New Zealand for making me give up this new part of my identity and definition of home that was connected to Canada. When I was in Canada I grew my identity to incorporate and enjoy my day-to-day life there. I absolutely loved it and I felt like this was the physical location where I could establish a long-term home that I was destined for. Yet at the same time I had for years and years wanted to be an air traffic controller and I was prepared to do anything to have the opportunity until I had my experience in Canada. It was more than an experience it was an identity and home defining experience which for a CBP is something you long for and search for in your life. It is a fulfilment that is at the forefront of your mind so when you find it, you do not want to give it up.

I was in Dubai when I got the news that I was accepted into air traffic control training and I was completely heartbroken because I was quietly hoping I would not get in so that I could go back to Canada. I selfishly was in tears on my mum's birthday when we went out for dinner at this fancy restaurant near the Burj Al Arab because I felt as if a part of who I am had once again been taken away from me. At that place in time, I thought Canada completed who I was, was my true home and made my identity feel whole. That was when my mum shared her life experience of moving to different countries and really explained that home can sometimes be a place in time. She shared with me all the places that she has felt she has had a home. She explained that each of these places are a part of who she is. These places include Colorado, Papua New Guinea, the Seychelles, Dubai and New Zealand, each for different reasons. Although for months after I returned to New Zealand to complete my training, which is what I wanted to do career wise, I missed my life in Canada. It was then that my mum's words started to become tools I used to patch together my definition of home. Canada was a place in time, it did feel like home but most importantly it has shown me what I really want out of life. I began patching together all my different definitions of home. Definitions that had been redefined over time as my life has changed. It was now time for me to redefine home again in this new era of life and after all this time of resentment towards New Zealand, I realised that what I had been looking for, I had all this time.

New Zealand

New Zealand has become a place I truly call home now, it is part of my cultural blend. It has taken many years to get to this point. When I moved to New Zealand in 2006 it was not a home at first because my only experiences in New Zealand had been on a few school holidays. I did not attach to any one town in New Zealand because I have moved multiple times. Due to this there was always a sense of rootlessness. I often felt upset that I was missing out on something that everyone else had so I clung to Dubai as my real home and subconsciously rejected the idea of allowing New Zealand to be called home. It was not until 2020 during the pandemic when I realised New Zealand was all I had because the day had finally come when my dad left Dubai for good. Until that year I never had to learn how to live without Dubai. It was almost like an addiction because I had to completely give it up to learn how to cope without it.

What I did not realise was that I was growing comforts in New Zealand that were slowly blending with my identity that I ignored. The reason I was not aware of it happening was because I was convinced that New Zealand was to blame for the disruption of my identity, home and understanding of where I was from. It was not until I realised that New Zealand was all I had that I began to reflect on everything I had in that moment and everything I have gained in my life. Defining home is realising what you want out of a home and what you want is subject to change as your life evolves. I realised at that point in time in 2020 that I have never settled anywhere in life because I have always had a reason to leave. I realised I did not have plans to leave anymore because I was growing my career here. I realised I wanted to settle here and call it home like the way I instantly did in Canada.

When I finally sat and worked through this attitude I have had towards New Zealand I realised that what I had been looking for was in

New Zealand this whole time, I just had to discover it. I finally escaped my fixation of thinking I needed to be like everyone else, that to be a real New Zealander I had to have lived here since I was born and have a pure Kiwi accent. I realised I did not have to be that way to fit in. New Zealand is my home in my own culturally blended way. It is the physical location that I do not have to leave after 30 days. It has the things I want in a home, it has snow, it has cities, and it has plenty of culturally blended people mixed throughout the population. New Zealand allows me the freedom to express my culturally blended way of life in whatever form I want. I finally realised that I had applied home as a state of mind and place in time everywhere except New Zealand and so in 2020 I implemented that theory again, defining home in New Zealand at last. I am a cultural blend of Dubai, the United States, New Zealand with a splash of Canada.

It is cliche to say this, but it rings true, home is where the heart is and that heart is beating inside of you right now. In a culturally blended way of life home is nomadic. It is as if you are a turtle and you carry home on your back. You may settle for a time but then you may move again. Just because a place is left does not mean all the things that make you feel at home are left behind to. They are all a part of the aura of you that is really a state of mind that you need to manifest allowing you to recreate, assimilate and blend home with new eras in your life. In this way you will keep adding twigs to your nest and create home in your own culturally blended way. The key to defining home is remembering that home is a state of mind, as well as a place in time. It is subject to change so allow it to evolve and appreciate each definition of home in each new era of your life and with each different place so that you live in the moment and are not overcome with homesickness.

Lorraine's Deep Dive of

DEFINING HOME

SPARKED BY OUR conversations I had with the lady on the bridge and the man in the café, Ashley and I began to discuss and search for a deeper understanding into what home means. The relationship between identity and one's sense of home is becoming one of increased complexity today. Researchers have noted that there is a clear connection between a person's idea of home and to their perception of their identity. This question *where are you from* is a question with inherent complexity to a Culturally Blended Person as it intertwines the place one would call home with their sense of their own personal identity. Culturally Blended People find that home transcends a physical location to a mindful connection. Home is a combination of places, experiences, sights, memories and people. Sometimes it is not fully tangible. Most of the time it is an invisible concept with real connections.

As I write this chapter I am at home in New Zealand. It is the middle of winter. It is the 22nd of June. Yesterday was the shortest day of the year. This morning I awoke to begin writing at 5:30 a.m. when it was still dark and cold outside. It will remain dark until after 8 a.m. when the sky will turn a dark grey as the forecast is for rain near the coast and more snow is expected in the mountains. When I first experienced a cold dark winter in the month of June in New Zealand, I had a deep sense of missing home. This feeling was repeated each time I experienced the cold dark winters in June and July in the southern hemisphere. There was a sense that something was missing. Cold, dark mornings have always been associated to me in my mind with December. Growing up in Colorado, and every year that I went back to visit, the Christmas tree lights cut through the dark mornings to twinkle colourful rays of magic in the home. This created a belonging feeling that wrapped itself warmly around me like a cosy blanket on a cold winter day.

Yesterday, I put up my Christmas tree in July to celebrate the southern hemisphere midwinter Christmas season. It is my way to feel that sense of home that I long for in the cold dark of winter. The Christmas tree that I put up connects me with more places than my childhood home in Colorado. Over the years of living in different countries, travelling and spending holidays with people from a variety of cultures, the tree is now decorated with ornaments gathered on my nomadic travels and in places that I have lived. Each ornament is connected to a time and a place that have become part of who I am, a connection, a sense of belonging, a feeling of home. Each ornament has a story that is woven into the story of me. This morning as I write, the Christmas tree that twinkles colour and warmth is a blend of home to me.

I recently read an article written by my friend Konstantina that she published on her Patreon site. She was writing in reflection to thoughts that she had on her rereading of Wilfred Thesiger's memoir titled Arabian Sands. It detailed the two crossings he did of the Empty Quarter, the expansive stretch of unbroken sand desert that has bested kings, adventurers and nomads for thousands of years. Konstantina shared that Thesiger addresses the sense of belonging that any avid traveller identifies with who has lived in foreign lands, embraced new cultures, and connected with diverse populations. During these crossings he spent time with nomads, people that do not define home by one particular geographical place on the map. Konstantina challenges our thinking in her article as today we have many modern-day nomads due to the unprecedented mobility of millions of people either for work or pleasure thanks to the global economy and the technological advancements of today. Konstantina reflects on her personal definition of home as a Greek and as a traveller and shares this, "With all my profound connection to my homeland Greece, I do not fully belong there anymore. I can sense that parts of my psyche are scattered in the world, stardust still hovering after the big bang. I sense an emotional attachment in unexpected places or with people I perceive to share little in common with which proves to me that I am retrieving lost pieces and am finally becoming whole again." Konstantina defines home as more than just a neighbourhood that she lives in but as a space independent of a specific physical location much like the nomads that Thesiger speaks about.

Home is connected to the community that we surround ourselves with that today includes both local communities and communities that are online. When I was younger and growing up in Colorado, my concept of community was the physical area that surrounded the home that I lived in. The community that I grew up in was composed of a couple of small towns that were connected to each other, where children from each town went to the same school and where events and traditions were held during the year. This is where I used to say that I was from as it referred to being from the community that I connected to. Today one's sense of community is not confined to a physical place as it was when I was growing up. Due to the connections we now readily have accessible to us through technological advancements in communication, community today exists physically in a local sense, virtually, and in a blend of both the virtual and physical worlds.

In 2006 when my daughters and I settled into the South Island in New Zealand I mentioned that we set up two homes, one in Dubai and one in New Zealand. These homes to myself, daughters and husband, were always seamlessly connected by Skype calls each day. It was common for Wayne to sit at the dining room table with us sometimes physically and more often virtually through Skype on the laptop that sat in his place. Whether Wayne was physically with us or virtually through a computer screen, he was still at home with us. Home is an aura, it is an atmosphere that can be recreated anywhere. The concepts and perceptions of home within community will continue to evolve. The global pandemic that the world was collectively thrust into in 2020 will forever be a point that redefines community in the traditional sense. The events of 2020 disconnected us as humans physically from each other as cities and countries went into lockdown confining people to the four walls that they lived in. As humans we have this innate desire to connect with other humans. Within a few short months into the 2020 pandemic a new verb was added to people's vocabulary around the world and that verb was Zooming. As people Zoomed together, connected on Zoom calls, they did not just do so for work meetings or family gatherings, but it exploded into other possibilities. Choirs were formed with people not in one place in a traditional sense of connection and community, but the voices came from all around the globe into one space, a Zoom space, that was recorded and shared for others to enjoy. The concept of community today is transforming and connecting us locally and globally.

As humans we seek to belong to a place we call home and to a community that home resides in. Today home can be your childhood roots and the pizzeria around the corner. Home can be the house you grew up in and the familiar sights, sounds, tastes, and smells that are familiar to you. It can be the physical place you reside in and the local community that surrounds it. It can be a virtual place where a community of likeminded people gather that are disconnected physically but still connected on a human level. Home can be the conversations with loved ones at the dinner table about anything and everything. Home can be time spent travelling creating memories that you carry with you much like a snail carries its home with him wherever he goes. Today the concept of home and where you belong and where you are from is evolving in our human search to connect in a world that allows us to venture and live outside of the place we were born. Home today is defined by you in the way that you sense, feel and understand it.

PART THREE

ASSIMILATING
to take in and fully absorb

8
CULTURAL CAULDRON

SATURDAY EVENING IN PRAGUE
Sunset from the Saint Nicholas Church

Lorraine

AFTER THE AMERICAN guy said his farewells at the groovy cafe we had met him in, Ashley started scrolling through her phone. She had a list of all the places that she still wanted to see before we left Prague. "We still need to check out Malá Strana which is on the other side of the Charles Bridge. There is a church there that apparently has great views of the castle on the hill and the city below. We can walk back that way and have dinner in that borough of Prague," Ashley said, and I nodded my head in agreement.

We spent the rest of the day strolling around Malá Strana dazzled by the Baroque and Renaissance styled buildings. They were all perfectly squished together and exhibited a range of proud and bold colours. This borough was becoming my favourite part of the city. It was nearing sunset and we still had one more thing to check off the list before dinner, the Saint Nicholas Church.

We stood on the front steps in awe of the church that rose above us in all her exquisite glory. It was remarkably beautiful and intricate on the inside with a predominant Baroque style along with adaptations from Gothic and Rococo styles. The city of Prague elegantly showcased an evolution and fusion of architecture that told a story of the city's rich history and diversity throughout the centuries. We found the staircase that led to the top balcony of the church. We followed the spiral stairs up, up and up towards the sky. After the dim climb up, at times feeling our way in partial darkness, we stepped out onto the balcony into the afternoon light. We were rewarded with a magical 360-degree view of the whole city. There is something special about high places. The bird's-eye view captures a different perspective and insight. We could see below all the speedy locals whizzing their way between the slow-paced tourists. A kaleidoscope of different people were all moving in their own direction yet seamlessly together. These showcased visually a significant metaphor to everything we had been talking about on this trip.

As we rested our elbows on the rails overlooking the city, we were treated to a spectacular sunset behind Prague Castle. We watched the sky change colours as if an artist was painting the scene. It was as if we were gazing up at the paintings on the ceilings of the church and being dazzled by their detail but this time the ceiling was the sky. There is something so magical about sunsets and how the colours blend together so seamlessly. You can never really tell where the colours start and where they end yet the distinction of colours is evidently visible. It was one perfect gradient of colours that collaborated together, blending beautifully, to create something so outstanding and distinctive.

After the sunset, the stars began twinkling against the blue-black sky. We were ready to enjoy a pizza and pint of Czech beer at one of the restaurants in Malá Strana. The smell of Italian food was wafting out into the street from a groovy restaurant near the church so we beelined for it. We were ushered inside and led to a table downstairs. Two frothy pints of Czech beer were placed in front of us as we waited for our pizzas. The atmosphere was dim and moody amid the lively conversation and twinkling ceiling lights. Something about this place felt magical as if we were among a world of witches and wizards.

Ashley was munching on some breadsticks that were placed on our table when I, always interested in my daughter's young perceptions of life, asked her, "So what is your take on all of this? We have spent the week discussing some heavy issues. How would you sum up your thoughts?" Ashley's glance moved towards the ceiling as she paused in thought for a moment. She grabbed the beer mug handle and took a big gulp and proceeded to dive into the details of this idea that was brewing in her mind that she named the Cultural Cauldron. Our pizzas soon arrived with a smile from the waiter. As we pulled our cheesy and stretchy pizza slices apart, I continued to listen as Ashley dived deeper into her metaphorical visual aid called the Cultural Cauldron.

Ashley's Deep Dive of

THE CULTURAL CAULDRON

ON OUR LAST evening in Prague, downstairs in the pizza restaurant, I leaned against the aged brown wood table with a gothic candle flickering between Mum and I and began sharing my Cultural Cauldron concept that had been brewing in the back of my mind since the start of our conversations on the trip. I love the fantasy of magic and I love how it is completely and utterly unexplainable yet so realistic. If I was to attend a school for witches and wizards my favourite class would be potions as it speaks worlds to my creativity and imagination. The murky but mysteriously exciting classroom bordered by dusty books of ancient, divine and unimaginable potion recipes is just the kind of place I would have excelled in. One would imagine that in potions class you are required to have a cauldron so for the purpose of this I ask that you visualise a cauldron.

The Cultural Cauldron concept is a metaphorical visual aid to help understand cultural blends personally and societally. Personally, it is used to understand your identity. Societally, it is used to understand the identity of communities and societies that are multicultural. What you pour into your cauldron are cultural potions that all swirl and brew together. Every culture has its own unique potion which has an original colour like no other. It may even include a liquid textile such as sparkles. It is completely up to your imagination. It can be as simple or as flamboyant as you would like it to be. There are no limits as to how many cultural potions can be poured into your personal cauldron and a societies cauldron. The ratio of each potion poured in is another fundamental part of this concept as different cultures have different degrees of influence on a person or on a society's identity. The overall blend of potions inside the cauldron is what I call the Ultimate Potion. The important fact to note is that the cultural potions swirl together yet retain their individuality. There is a fear that mixing cultures may cause individual cultures within to become diluted and indistinguishable. This is not the case in terms of the Cultural Cauldron concept. Cultures swirl together, alongside one another but retain their individuality so you can see each colour of the potion clearly while still being blended and a part of all the others. This is the beauty of how cultural blends are represented both personally and societally.

Personally

Visualise an empty cauldron in front of you. Inside the cauldron is where the ever-brewing magic happens that represents your cultural identity. Throughout your life you pour cultural potions, the cultures that you identify with, into your ever brewing cauldron which creates the Ultimate Potion of your identity. Again, the most powerful and important fact to recognise is that each potion retains its individuality while swirling with the others. It could be thought that a multicultural person is the exact same as another multicultural person as when many colours blend together they look the same. This is, however, not the case as each person has different colours of potions they are pouring into their cauldron and therefore the blend for each multicultural person will be magically different.

I will use myself as an example. Imagine that you are looking into my cauldron that is heating up over a small fire in the centre of the room. Into that cauldron I begin pouring in a purple potion that represents the United Arab Emirates. I now pour in a blue potion with red sparkles that represents the United States of America. You can see how the purple and blue sparkly red potions are blending side by side, but they retain their distinct colours. Next, I pour in the lime green potion that represents New Zealand. Watch as the three potions all swirl together but still retain their individual colours. We witness the changing patterns with every second as the cauldron slowly swirls its contents. Following an interlude of gazing at the creation of my Ultimate Potion I pick up the cherry-red potion that represents Canada. This is a smaller part of my identity so I just pour in a little drop of this potion. Now there are a mix of four, all in different ratios, that are blending together seamlessly yet retaining their individuality as we can clearly see the purple, blue sparkly red, lime green, and cherry-red potions.

Your Cultural Cauldron is ever brewing and ever evolving. Just like it has been mentioned throughout this book, everything in life changes and nothing stays the same. As your identity changes throughout different periods of your life, the potions in your Cultural Cauldron will also change in ratio through addition and subtraction as your identity changes depending on influences by different cultures. For example, there were only three potions swirling in my cauldron before I moved to Canada. Canada is not where I am from but it holds a significant and symbolic place in my Cultural Cauldron as my experience in Canada has blended into my identity. It was after 20 years that I added in a dash of Canada, that has evolved my Ultimate Potion into something different from what it was a year ago. That is the flexibility that comes with the nature of the Cultural Cauldron concept as you become continuously influenced and uninfluenced by different cultures throughout your life.

The Cultural Cauldron concept is the perfect visual aid to fully understand your culturally blended identity if you are struggling to define what it looks like. In this way you can realise that you do not have to compartmentalise who you are in different situations. When you compartmentalise yourself it is as if visually you have a different cauldron for each culture you relate to. This would mean that there is only one potion in each cauldron instead of a blend which is the true you. If you compartmentalise who you are then you will have a constant underlying feeling that you are missing the other parts of your identity. The important fact to note is that at the end of the day you are truly a blend that cannot be separated because if you do separate yourself then there will be a feeling of emptiness from denying who you truly are. The Ultimate Potion reflects your blended, unique and distinct identity.

Now I implore you to visualise the cultures significant to your identity and imagine them as potions. Pour their differing ratios into your own cauldron and see what your ultimate potion looks like. Remember they are blended together but retain their individual colours, highlighting the fact that the identity of a culturally blended person is not an indistinguishable mesh of cultures that together blend to produce one colour. The purpose of this is to give confidence to Culturally Blended People that their identity is not something bland, confusing and with no distinguishability. This occurs particularly in a case where you do not identify with the entirety of a culture yet it still holds a significant part of who you are.

Societally

Countries, cultures and societies throughout history have formed, dissolved, assimilated and changed in their societal identity. Societies within countries and cultures have continued to evolve and blend. Since the beginning of time, people have moved across the river, over the hill, into the next town, into the next country and to another continent. People have taken their identity with them and have over time begun to blend it in with the culture of the new place.

The same process applies with a society's cauldron as with one's personal cauldron. The identity of a society is made up of different ratios of each cultural potion where they swirl together yet retain individuality like the gradient of colours in a sunset. It is important that people who are part of a multicultural society remain open to the natural change and flow that evolution brings to a culture. People should not be hesitant to allow new people to bring their cultures, or blend of cultures, into the society. There can be a hesitation to incorporate the likes of refugees, immigrants, expats or anyone that is presumably different because it is easy to assume that the original society and culture may become indistinguishable, unrecognisable, diluted and will lose its uniqueness. People can become afraid that they will lose their national identity and heritage if too many people from different cultures are added into the mixing pot. They fear that eventually the original culture will be forgotten. People can also assume that foreigners are going to grow pockets of their own culture within the country, instead of integrating and respecting the culture within the country they have come to. It is understandable that they will gravitate to a group like themselves as they will find security, comfort, and a sense of home. It is important in societies today, in our world that is globally connected, to allow people who move into a new culture to find easy ways to integrate and redefine home in the new place. By not making it easy for them they will want to find a comfortable place to exist which can create secluded and segregated pockets inside of a society. The important fact to remember is that by being open to the natural evolution of societies a dilution of a culture will not happen but all cultures of a society will swirl together as one while retaining their individuality and uniqueness. A society can successfully become a cultural blend when there is acceptance involved. This will create a societal Cultural Cauldron with its own unique Ultimate Potion which is made of all the contributing cultural potions that are blended together yet remain distinguishable. It retains the original culture but is inclusive of the others so that they are all connected allowing the society to blend together and be cooperative without stereotypes and misunderstandings.

There is a restaurant in Dubai that my family and I love going to. On the menu it has the standard meal sections including appetisers, mains, sharing, sides and desserts. On each page there is one side that is a Western version which includes food like burgers, burritos and roasts and on the other side there is the Eastern version which includes foods like rice, noodles and kebabs. These two global versions are side by side but under the same meal section. Each plate brings out wonderful flavours and elements specific to the cultures they originated from but at the end of the day it is all part of the same menu. Each dish is meant to be enjoyed with the other dishes. It is in this way that different cultures within one society can coexist, blend and still retain their individuality. In actual fact, it was at this restaurant that Mum and I decided to commit to writing this book after recognising the hidden significance of the menu.

Each society has its own cauldron and each CBP has their own cauldron in which various ratios of potions swirl together. Each society is a whole entity but consists of a blend of potions that create a united, respectful, culturally mindful, powerful and wise society. Each person is a whole entity but consists of a blend of potions that represents their culturally blended identity. It is important to continuously remember that the cultural potions swirl together yet retain their individuality and do not dilute one or the other. It is in this way that we achieve the perfect balance of being able to distinguish the cultures within while watching as they brew and blend together as one product, one Ultimate Potion.

9

GLOBAL MINDSET

SUNDAY MORNING IN PRAGUE
Walk Along Vltava River

Ashley

WITH A COFFEE each that we ordered from PAUL's bakery, we popped out of a twisty lane and onto a walkway bordering the main road by the Vltava River. We crossed the road and joined the light procession of strolling tourists and locals on the sidewalk. Today was our last day in Prague as we would be flying out tomorrow afternoon. The takeaway coffees were keeping our fingers toasty warm while the steam rose and warmed our faces.

This was the coolest morning, temperature wise since our arrival in Prague. The fact that it was early on a Sunday morning and that it was quite cool meant that there were fewer people strolling the streets. It was a welcome change from the busy and bustling days that we had experienced during the week prior. The added peacefulness allowed us to notice the small things like the swan being chased by her fluffy cygnets in the current of the dark green river. In the distance we heard someone busking, the melodic song being sung in Czech. We walked past fellow tourists and locals of all cultures. The diversity that we were surrounded by was delightfully on brand with our discussions over the past week that had touched on so many different aspects of being a Culturally Blended Person.

We thought about the children, teenagers, adults and parents of today that all experience and face similar issues to the ones that we had uncovered this past week. We agreed that without understanding one's uniqueness as a Culturally Blended Person they too will suffer the lack of clarity of who they are especially when asked the question *where are you from.*

After bouncing issues and solutions back and forth we agreed that there needs to be more awareness created. I said to Mum, "People need to have a different mindset. That is what needs to change." "This is true," Mum agreed, "people need to adopt a global mindset."

We discussed that a global mindset was not just for people that considered themselves cultural blends but is a mindset for anyone. It can include a person who has never travelled overseas, a person who has grown up in one culture their whole life yet has an interest in the diversity and cultural blends that we find everywhere in today's world.

Our conversation was interrupted by the sound of church bells that began to chime and were heard throughout the city. The musical notes transcended the buildings and filled the mellow morning with sound. It reminded me of the call to prayer in Dubai as both are heard throughout the city. Everyone can hear the chimes regardless of what they are doing and where they are. A global mindset is as if everyone hears the same church bells or the same call to prayer. They individually, yet together, become aware of the connectedness that we all have in our world. A global mindset is that unified understanding that persists in the way that we perceive our world and our place in it.

Ashley's Deep Dive of

GLOBAL MINDSET

A GLOBAL MINDSET refers to an openness to learn, to adapt and perceive diversity within cultures and people. A global mindset can be nurtured with or without travel as resources for learning are found through many means such as experiencing it first-hand, having conversations and searching about it online. To explain how to practice a global mindset in terms of culture I will introduce the concept of being on the inside looking around, instead of on the outside looking in. This is a tool that people can use to widen their cultural peripherals and enhance their cultural wisdom.

To set the visual scene for this tool I want you to imagine that there is an encircled fence with a gate that has fog floating in front of it. To be on the inside is where a global mindset is created, evolved and shared. To be on the outside is where perceptions are distorted, narrowed and the truth is not the whole truth. Being on the outside of the gate is also where people who have been secluded from a culture stand.

Being on the inside looking around instead of on the outside looking in means one has walked through the gate of the culture and is able to observe it from within. A person will have a full 360-degree view of its reality and perceptions educated from within the culture without bias or personal opinions preventing a true understanding. When you are on the inside looking around you immerse yourself within the core of the culture and can gain clarity on why a culture is the way that it is and you will be wiser in terms of realising the actions and logic behind the people of a culture.

A person who is on the inside looking around instead of the outside looking in also holds the responsibility of not making someone else feel stupid or ignorant because they do not know certain things about cultures, countries, religions and social etiquettes. It is not fair to fault someone if they have presumptuous stereotypes or opinions because they probably have never had anyone else give them a real perspective. Having a global mindset means that we are also leaders in having conversations with people about cultures to open their minds to the richness in our diversity today. It is in this way that we expand other people's mindsets like the domino effect. If you find yourself in the presence of someone who is on the outside of a gate looking in at the distorted fog, then take the initiative to teach them or even learn together about the particular culture in a positive way. In this way cultural peripherals will be widened.

Being on the outside looking in means one is gaining a perception from being on the outside of a culture. I have noticed that ill-thought-out perspectives, biased news and stereotypes act as a fog that floats outside the gate that prohibits people seeing the reality of a culture. This fog obscures the truth behind a culture's traditions, history and people. These perspectives, biased news and stereotypes have a degree of truth to them as they are either formulated from an elaborate or literal truth. Yet sometimes they are believed to be the only truth which makes the fog reluctant to lift hiding the existence of a gate that could be opened so one can walk inside the culture to learn the truth. When people are on the outside looking in, the result is that those people learn about the culture from stereotypes and opinions from people not within the culture. People gain a perspective that is distorted instead of the perspectives and point of view from within the culture itself.

There are two main reasons that people are found on the outside looking in at the closed gate of a culture. Exploring these will help people understand what the reason is that is prohibiting yourself or others from being on the inside looking around. When this is recognised, you can take the initiative to guide yourself and other people through the fog, open the gate and gain access to being on the inside looking around at a culture. By taking this initiative for yourself and for others you are widening yours and their peripherals, enhancing cultural wisdom, and furthering a global mindset.

Firstly, people are on the outside when they either feel rejected to participate in a culture or are viewed as someone that could dilute the purity of a culture. People in a society need to recognise that by limiting their culture to a specific ethnicity and/or nationality creates pockets in societies. It is important to realise that this is not a case of 'too much cabbage ruins the sauerkraut' (I don't know if that's true, but it was something a friend of mine often said and I think the theory of that applies here). It is actually a case of 'two different packets of M&Ms just means more M&Ms'. If people are not allowed to be on the inside looking around at the root of the culture and understand it from a real perspective they are going to judge it from the fog that floats outside the gate. In this way ethnicities, cultures and nationalities will not see eye to eye. By opening the gate and allowing others in we can build a bridge of understanding which will promote the idea of a Cultural Cauldron in a society where all cultures are blended together yet retain their individuality. This is a change in perception from a group of people culturally different from the presumed original culture who should not be perceived as diluting that culture. By allowing people inside they will gain wisdom and cultural clashes can be overcome enhancing global mindsets. It also nurtures and promotes culturally diverse communities where there is respect and understanding without borders.

Secondly, people may be on the outside because they are a person who is not receptive to another culture. There are people who do not know how to think outside of the culture they currently live in when learning about other cultures. There is also a population of people that are innocently oblivious to another way of life. When a person is not provided with an environment to widen their cultural peripherals or if the information they are receiving is prohibiting any kind of positive inclusivity and honest understanding of a culture, then they will naturally not want to open the gate because it feels foreign or even scary to them. This intensifies the fog in front of the gate.

There will always be a population of people who want to keep the gates of other cultures closed as they do not want to learn about anything outside of their norm. They may also have an ideology that their culture is the correct one. The best way to encourage a global mindset is to have open-minded and peaceful conversations with people in this category. It is our responsibility to lead others to move inside the gate and to look around through conversation. This will help to expand a person's cultural peripherals to become knowledgeable of other perspectives. By both being led and taking the lead it will enable a more peaceful global environment where the fog is lifted and the gates are open. It is in this way that we can turn cultural clashes into respected cultural differences.

Adopting a global mindset requires us to be on the inside looking around at a culture instead of being on the outside looking in. The act of opening the gate and walking inside of a culture to look around is an initiative one must make as well as an initiative one should encourage others to make. As a Culturally Blended Person, I have the opportunity to be on the inside looking around at the cultures that my identity is connected to. When I meet another person, instead of relying on half-truths and stereotypes, I approach that person with a global mindset, with a desire and willingness to learn from their point of view and personal experience.

I will share a couple of stories with you showcasing the presence of a global mindset with an appreciation and awareness of Culturally Blended People. This will also detail how one can be on the inside looking around at a culture with or without travelling which exemplifies that a global mindset can be gained through all kinds of means and is open to everyone.

During 2016 and 2017, I worked at a Cambodian restaurant in Wellington, New Zealand. I was familiar with the part of the world known as Southeast Asia, yet I was not familiar with each country within the region. In fact, I had never actually heard of Cambodia before working at that Cambodian restaurant. My experience of working at that restaurant opened my eyes to the life and culture in Cambodia. I learned a great deal from my fellow employees that were born in Cambodia and moved to New Zealand. In fact, the owner and his mother were refugees during the Pol Pot regime. My employers did not talk too much about what happened during that specific part of history, only snippets, which I respected. I learnt about their culture while sitting with them after we had closed, eating leftover Cambodian food from the night amid the Cambodian music and decor of the restaurant. It was a wonderful time after the rush of the day to feel as if I was on the inside looking around and enriching my global mindset from these Culturally Blended People. The owner had a strong, hearty Kiwi accent and portrayed classic Kiwi humour whereas his wife had more of a Cambodian accent but sprinkled with common Kiwi phrases. His wife's sister, who constantly claimed New Zealand as home, had a tiny hint of a Cambodian accent and the owner's mother did not converse in English often. Among this culturally blended family they were each different even though they experienced similar circumstances. This highlights the fact that even among families it cannot be assumed how each member feels or what they identify with as everyone's experience and elements of home and identity are different. If we look at the owner and his mother for a short case study, he appeared to be more of a Kiwi from an outsider's perspective whereas his mother rarely talked in English, yet she was the one that brought her son to New Zealand and settled him into Kiwi culture. She made New Zealand home for him while recreating Cambodian culture and homely elements in New Zealand. They each spent the same amount of time in New Zealand yet were different in their own stories and identity. This is the beauty and diversity of Culturally Blended People. While working there I gained more wisdom about a culture I did not know about, as well as being among other Culturally Blended People. It was a very heart-warming time of my life, a time of learning about another culture from the inside engaging in conversation.

During my time working there I expanded my global mindset to people, places and beliefs that were not familiar to me. It was in this way that my perceptions were not being distorted by the fog on the outside of the gate which is an experience I am so lucky to have had without having to travel overseas. This exemplifies the point that you do not need to be a Culturally Blended Person yourself to be able to have a global mindset because perceptions and cultural appreciation can be gained without having to travel.

On another occasion in that Cambodian restaurant, I witnessed the presence of a desire to cultivate a global mindset shared by a customer. One evening I was serving a large table of sophisticated women and men. As I was placing everyone's dishes in front of them, I overheard a conversation between a few of the customers. "So, you just came back from Southeast Asia, tell us about that," one woman asked the man she was sitting next to at the table. He began sharing stories about the adventures he and his family had while touring around the various countries within that corridor of Asia. Another women on the opposite side of the table said, "I love how you travel with your kids, what do you call those trips again?" The man replied, "Cultural cruises." He explained that it was important to him and his wife to give their children an opportunity to experience a world outside of New Zealand. He knew that this would encourage them to grow up to be respectful of other people and cultures which he felt was important to their development. I smiled as I walked away from their table as I thought about what that dad had said and found it to be so incredible. He and his wife valued enriching their children's lives as well as themselves by having diverse cultural experiences. When people choose options like this it becomes the momentum required to open the gates of understanding between cultures and countries. Those parents are encouraging both themselves and their children to create and enhance their global mindset by travelling, yet that is not the only way a global mindset can be achieved. It can also be effectively achieved by having conversations at the dinner table about the differences in our world in an unbiased way where a global mindset can be gained while still at home.

A Kiwi friend of mine who grew up in New Zealand spent her last year of high school in Sweden. While there she learnt how to speak Swedish and lived with a Swedish family. She started to integrate, grow accustomed to and became a part of the Swedish culture. Despite not being Swedish and not considering Sweden as where she is from, her thoughts, actions, respect and wisdom will forever have a Swedish influence on her character as a whole. She created memories and friendships there, as well as a connection to Sweden that is now intertwined with her aura of how she sees the world and herself. She was able to learn about Sweden from the inside looking around and by doing so this has assisted her to expand her global mindset.

Another memory and example I recall happened on a beautiful day; it was the first of July 2018. I was in Whistler, Canada and people were out in the sunny warm weather celebrating Canada Day. I was unfortunately working so I did not get to participate in all the festivities. It was during the quiet lunch shift when an American family came in for a refreshing drink and short break from the sun. As I was serving them their drinks the dad lifted up his beer and said, "Cheers family to Canada Day!" The mum beamed and picked up her glass when one of their younger daughters asked, "Dad, why are we celebrating Canada Day if we are American?" Her dad replied, "We are celebrating Canada Day because we are in Canada and it is an important tradition and holiday for them. It does not matter what nationality we are. It is respectful to celebrate a different nation's tradition when visiting their country."

That was such a touching conversation to overhear and it will forever be a beautiful memory. Everyone reading this book should take away the advice that father gave to his daughter. Celebrate because it is respectful. That dad was encouraging his family to be on the inside looking around by participating in a national tradition despite not being Canadian themselves. It is an important cultural lesson for children and adults to support other countries regardless of their own nationality. It is not any different from the famous saying when in Rome do as the Romans do. By having this value as a person, you will enhance your cultural peripherals, cultural wisdom and global mindset.

Another experience I had also happened when I was in Canada. It occurred in the wintry months of early 2018. I was working in the ski rental shop on a snowy day. A Lebanese man came in to get his skis and boots fitted as he was going to brave the weather. As we chatted, he asked me where I was from. I gave him my whole spiel about being raised in Dubai while being an American and a New Zealander. We had a lovely conversation about Dubai because he was thinking about moving there. A week later I was working at the station that collects the used equipment. The same Lebanese man came in to drop his gear off and as I was scanning the equipment he asked, "Do you remember me?" I looked up and said, "Oh yes! You are from Lebanon." Then he replied, "Yes! And you are from Dubai!" Having had so many people throughout my life disagree with me whenever I would say that I am from Dubai this moment was so very special. Not only was I recognised for the place I believe I am truly from, but I was recognised as being from Dubai by a Middle Eastern person when I thought I would never be accepted as being part of their world.

This goes to show that there is evidence of people in this world with a global mindset who show openness and understanding to people like me, a Culturally Blended Person. This concept of learning about cultures from being on the inside looking around, instead of the outside looking in, is a useful tool when it comes to understanding each other's cultural differences and better yet, respecting those differences. We are all human; we are all Homo sapiens. The word sapiens is derived from sapience which means wisdom. We are creatures of wisdom. It is our opportunity and our challenge to live up to that standard. It is very easy to be wise in terms of widening your cultural peripherals. It is in this way that you can develop and grow your global mindset with or without travel.

Lorraine's Deep Dive of

GLOBAL MINDSET

I GREW UP with three television stations, not television sets, and I did not have a cell phone that gave me access to learning about other parts of the world in an instant. I remember the first time I learned about people personally outside of my local environment was when I was involved in a classroom project in school whereby each student chose and corresponded with a pen pal from another country. It was through this snail mail correspondence that I first remember learning personally about another way of living and another culture.

When I was growing up, we did not travel as a family. There was only a couple times that we went beyond our town and nearby city, most often to visit relatives in California. However, my dad raised me to always be curious. He asked me questions and encouraged me to ask questions. I was encouraged to explore and to learn new things by venturing out of my comfort zone, to not be afraid of fear or mistakes. I was encouraged to seek my own solutions to problems and as I grew up my dad stepped away, not in an act of non-support, but to allow me the opportunity to develop independent thinking. Curiosity and the ability to deal with situations that might not be entirely familiar or clear are the drivers for global thinkers. We are stimulated by the world and by our environment. I grew up in an environment whereby I did not shrink away from difference, diversity or foreign circumstances but learned to thrive in it. I raised my daughters with the same values that my dad and mom raised me. The point that is necessary to highlight is that I did not travel or move beyond my home base when I was young, yet I was raised to think globally. Living abroad and travelling is not a necessary element to having a global mindset because technology today allows us to learn, interact and connect so easily.

A normal part of my children's upbringing was to have a world map clearly displayed in the house in Dubai. The primary reason was so that each night we could play the game Where in the World is Dad? As an international pilot, Wayne could be anywhere in the world. This game had variations that included locating grandparents, aunties and uncles, and friends that were living in a different country or had returned to their country of citizenship. The most important impact that this map had on the mindset of my children was that they understood visually that they were part of a global community of people, diverse and connected. As a mother it was very important to me to ensure that they knew that they were a valued part of the global community in which they belonged. Little did I know then that in the years ahead this would also play a part in how they defined their identity. Little did any of us know in the early 2000s how fast our world would become connected through travel and technology.

Our world is now a place where having a global mindset is easy to have. It requires us to simply make the choice to seek out ways to connect and learn from each other. The degree of interactions across many cultural lines has never happened to this degree in the history of humankind. Even for those that have not grown up in a multicultural environment nor have had the opportunity to travel, they still have 24/7 access to our globally connected world. A person in a village in Nigeria can easily be watching the same video, live or recorded, as someone else in New York City, as well as another person travelling on a train in Bangkok. Each can watch the video, comment and interact through conversation. Developing a global mindset is now a focus found in many school curriculums as it is clear that our youth of today will need such an understanding. A global mindset allows the young generation to develop skills that are needed in our diverse world.

Today we learn about other cultures through the conversations that we have with others and also through the sharing of art, dance and music. I have noted that certain cities are celebrating their diversity by hosting events and festivals with cultural themes. As well, we now have 24-hour access through our communication channels with platforms such as YouTube to witness the blending of cultures. I recently listened to a YouTube video of a man who was playing a didgeridoo, an Australian aboriginal wind instrument, in a piece of jazz music. Clear cultural integration was heard on this video. As well, during the Covid-19 home isolation that many of us experienced we shared together in music, theatre and art as choirs sang, musicians played, and museum doors opened for us all to have a virtual front seat in experiencing diversity in culture. It was done online primarily for entertainment, but it has a more profound effect.

In the beginning of 2020 when much of the world was experiencing a lock down situation, Airbnb offered new online experiences. Of course, with much of the world in lock down the people that had previously offered personal experiences could no longer offer them. Airbnb quickly adapted and began offering online experiences. It was in April when Ashley and I both signed up with a local Prague man who was offering a virtual tour of Prague through Airbnb experiences. It was very special for Ashley and me to once again be in the streets of

Prague as one Zoom window was our eyes as if we were really there. We joined people from different parts of the world on this virtual tour all travelling together and enjoying great conversations. A few of us had been to Prague before and were able to chime in with our stories and compare notes. We learned about each other and learned more about the city from our host, a local man from Prague. Today technology allows us to connect on a deeper level to learn about our world and the people in it. However, I do need to point out that it is a choice that people need to make. Just because the technology that we have today allows us easily to learn about the rich diversity of people and their cultures in our world today, it will not happen unless we make a choice to do so.

Today it is important that we foster conversations that embrace our rich diversity as people in our families and workplaces, in schools, in communities, both locally and online. A global mindset celebrates diversity and respects the differences and uniqueness of people. Our world today is a colourful cauldron of identities blending richly together. These identities can be found in the blends in our cities and communities. These identities can be found within one person, a Culturally Blended Person. As we look through the global mindset lenses, we see a colourful world distinct and blended harmoniously.

The best way to learn about viewpoints is to ask people for their perspectives. As I wanted to learn more about the different thoughts that people have about global mindset I searched and read good articles on the internet. I also asked people from different backgrounds and professions to share their idea on what a global mindset means to them. Below I have shared parts of these conversations that give you a wider view of thoughts then just the ones that I have been sharing.

Sep works professionally in the field of emotional and cultural intelligence and pushes to have concepts related to our world cultures and our global mindset taught more in schools. She emphasises that a global mindset is important for young people today who are preparing for their future. Sep shares that, "Children who are encouraged to develop their emotional and cultural intelligence will become more self-aware of their identity in a global world. They will become positive contributors in society."

Saira shares that in her view the world is a far smaller place when you are raised in a multicultural environment. She shares, "People that are raised with an openness to different cultures and to people that are cultural blends are able to more easily accept differences and are far more tolerant. These people often form deep bonds with people that are distinctly different from themselves yet understand the common bonds that tie them together as humans."

Rachel shares that part of a global mindset is seeing your country and culture from the outside. She explains, "There is a great benefit to having the vantage point of living in another country and seeing through the eyes of someone from another country. It is especially valuable to view the perception of your culture and country from the outside. It is also equally as valuable to view another culture from the inside. It shows you just how interwoven the world is and the importance of learning how to see everyone's perspectives even if you might disagree with them."

Samir shares, "The more cultures that I have adopted the easier it has become to connect to others authentically. A multicultural lifestyle cultivates resiliency in thinking and problem-solving that can give one an edge today both personally and professionally."

Anki mentions, "Having a global mindset has allowed me to be more accepting and understanding of the differences that exist among us and the similarities that unite us."

Having a global view or mindset allows you to see more than one side of an issue and allows you to get comfortable with the idea that there are not necessarily essential right and wrong ways of doing things. Many times, there are just different ways of doing the same things. Perceptions are just that, perceptions, not based on fact but on viewpoint. When our view is limited to only our way of thinking and doing things these become only our perceptions, or should I say misconceptions, of fully understanding.

In studies that identify qualities of global leaders, inquisitiveness or curiosity is seen as an essential quality. Inquisitiveness is a state of mind, an attitude rather than a skill. The reason that this is a quality sought after in leadership is because being curious about the world helps to cope with uncertainty and to balance contrasting cultural issues that are ever-present around us today.

To develop a global mindset that is open to cultural diversity starts with fostering self-awareness. To be self-aware simply means to pay attention to what you are thinking, how you are acting, how you are feeling and how you make decisions. You are stepping out of your situation and realising that how you act, what you do and how you feel is based on values and ideas that you have.

Anyone can have a global mindset. It is in fact, your choice.

PART FOUR

OWNING
to embrace the story of you

10

YOUR STORY

MONDAY MORNING IN PRAGUE
Returning to Dubai

Lorraine

WHAT A WEEK it had been, I thought. Ashley and I finished packing and headed downstairs to reception. I suggested that we take a taxi back to the airport instead of clambering back on the train and the bus. Ashley nodded with relief. I paid the bill and the receptionist at the boutique hotel ordered our chariot to the airport.

The taxi arrived and we hopped inside. We pulled into the stream of traffic and headed off towards the airport. I started a conversation with the driver and asked him, "Where in Czechoslovakia are you from?" The taxi driver replied in accented English, "We are the Czech Republic now, not Czechoslovakia. We split from Slovakia and are two individual countries today." Then the taxi driver told us about the 'velvet divorce' in 1989. This term refers to the split of the former country Czechoslovakia into the now two individual countries, the Czech Republic and Slovakia.

I had made a common mistake in calling the country Czecho-slovakia, a term I was familiar with from history class when I was at school. This new-found knowledge that the country split, especially one where a war was not declared, was something that escaped my knowledge. It was particularly interesting and special to have a local citizen explain this historical event to us from his perspective. The most powerful stories are the ones that are authentically shared. We had been privileged to meet people during our week in Prague that allowed us to learn about different perspectives by listening to their authentic stories.

Ashley commented quietly to me, "This is another country that has split which further shows how indefinite country borders are at any given time. If countries split for peaceful or non-peaceful reasons it further justifies that one's answer to the question *where are you from* can be forever changing given that its meaning can have multifaceted interpretations." This taxi driver would have grown up saying he was from Czechoslovakia. Now would he say that he was from Czechoslovakia or is he from the Czech Republic? A strange situation if he says the country he was born in and where most would say he is from is naming a place that no longer exists. I wondered if he still identified with the two countries as one or is happy to identity only with the Czech Republic. Whatever his answer is, it is the right one for him despite technicalities because it is his identity and his choice in defining it.

Once out of the main traffic and heading closer to the airport the taxi driver shared his personal story of growing up in a little country town in the region that belongs to the Czech Republic. He spoke in accented English and shared with us what it was like for him to move to Prague when he was a young adult. He remarked that he feels as if he belongs in Prague now, not in the little country town he grew up in. He said with a jolly laugh, "I didn't like the pigs," referring to the fact he prefers the city life over farm life. Ashley chuckled and her head was nodding in agreement. Arriving at the airport our driver pulled into the taxi lane to drop us off. The taxi driver bid farewell with a jovial final comment. "Enjoy your flight but why would you ever want to leave Prague? The food is good, and the beer is premier! You ladies have a lovely flight!"

It was one in the morning Dubai time when we began our descent into the city surrounded by desert. I looked over at Ashley and she was gazing out the window at the Burj Khalifa twinkling among all the other city lights. It had been an amazing trip. Somehow, I sensed that our conversations would continue. Once we had all our things and had cleared customs, we walked through the glossy glass doors into the sauna heat of Dubai. We got in the taxi line and the next thing I heard was, "Ma'am, Ma'am!!" A small Filipino women dressed in pink came racing towards us from the pink taxi line. The pink taxis in Dubai were just that, covered in pink paint. They were taxis just for women which was a normal aspect of Dubai day-to-day life. I could not believe it as I turned around to be greeted with a big hug. It was Cena, the lady that had helped our family when the girls were babies. Cena had stopped working for us after the girls and I moved to New Zealand. We kept in regular contact with her and knew that she was working as a taxi driver now. This was such a heart-warming coincidence because Cena was a very important part of our lives as a family. We spent the entire taxi trip back to our home in Dubai, where we did not even have to tell her our address, catching up with all of Cena's news and sharing ours with her. The ride home in Cena's pink taxi was such a nice touch after the week we had in Prague. Cena drove down Sheik Zayed Road through the sparkling city lights as a gaggle of great conversation and giggling filled the car, just like old times.

I had come to learn from the week that we spent in Prague that my now adult daughter had a different perception of her past than I had imagined. I was so thankful for the opportunity to openly discuss and to learn more about who she is and the story that she has to tell. This in turn made me reflect deeper, more internally, on myself and how my experiences have created my unique story.

Everything that happened during this week seemed to be perfectly placed as if it were magic. It was as if the world knew we needed to have conversations, share our experiences, learn from each other, write about our experiences and analyse the concepts behind tackling the question *where are you from*. It seemed to be clear in that moment that our story was to be written and shared so that we could reach out and extend a hand to others in similar situations. It was clear that we wanted to give others the encouragement and comfort of telling their own unique stories as Culturally Blended People in their own words.

Ashley's Deep Dive of

YOUR STORY

THE QUESTION *WHERE are you from* is really just meant to be a greeting as an introduction. It is not intentionally meant to cause internal confusion yet it still does for a significant number of people. Within the question *where are you from* the term *from* is both meaningful and meaningless. The question *where are you from* is insignificant to a certain population of people as it does not trigger any kind of insecurity in their identity. However, to people who define who they are and where they are from with more than one place then this question continues to strike a chord of difficulty whenever it is asked.

I can confidently tell you that there is no fill in the blank algorithm that we have kept until the very last chapter. The answer to the question of *where are you from* is simply knowing your story which is unique to you.

My mum shared with you the story early in this book about the homework I was given in primary school in Dubai where I had to write an essay titled *Where Are You From*. At seven years old I did not know what that meant so in a way to translate the concept of *where are you from* to a child my mum told me to write my story. Stories and fairy tales are a primary source of how children learn to speak and read so that is the way my mum decided to explain this question to me back then. Telling your story and more importantly how much of that story you want to tell someone is the answer to the question *where are you from*. Stories are how people learn and it is probably the most effective, captivating and spellbinding way to learn and educate a point of view throughout all the ages.

This final chapter is set as a task for you to think about how you want to write your story from start to present identifying all the things that have influenced your sense of belonging, definitions of home, definitions of the word *from*, and your culturally blended identity. Where you are from is not one geographical place but is a lifetime of influences. Your story is what you choose to embrace. You could be born with three citizenships, be a combination of five ethnicities and have lived in seven countries but they mean nothing until you make the choice of what you choose to embrace.

I encourage you to understand why you are the way that you are through introspection by relating yourself to the concepts brought up in this book to aid you in searching, discovering, assimilating, and owning your journey. Be confident in your culturally blended identity, your Ultimate Potion. Be confident in your story and you will find that what others say and what others think to oppose who you are will no longer affect you. Don't worry if you find that the question may still bother you, it still bothers me sometimes. When you are asked the question *where are you from* the task for you is to identify the situation that the question is being asked in and choose which parts of your story you want to say. Not everyone has to know your full story each time as that is the power you hold. You don't need to tell everyone your whole story, chapter to chapter. You can even start from the last chapter and work your way backwards to the first chapter if you feel that the last chapter, the one you are currently living in, best represents where you are from and your identity in that moment. Be selective about telling your story because questioning conversations that may leave you questioning yourself will not serve you. What you want is to have meaningful conversations with people where wisdom is shared so identify situations when a conversation like that is possible. Be confident in knowing that by only telling a part of your story it is not denying and shadowing the part of your identity that you are not telling as long as you are proud of your entire story.

A diamond forms under pressure. Since the time you first became unsure about where you are from you would have felt a pressure to answer the question and to please the questioner. As well, you might have felt a pressure to change yourself after your honest answer was not accepted. By nature diamonds are very strong. By being confident in your story you are creating a strong diamond that is unbreakable by misunderstood perceptions and follow-up questions questioning your identity, belonging, and where you are from. Remember that you are a culturally blended diamond that is strong and valuable.

I worked at the ice cream parlour in Whistler, Canada during the summer of 2018. During a staff meeting and get together, as there had been a bunch of new staff employed, we sat in a circle eating ice cream. There was a hat with questions in it placed in the middle which was going to be used for an ice-breaker game. A new girl that had been hired picked a question out of the hat first. From talking to her earlier I learned that she was born in China and has lived in China, Saudi Arabia, Denmark and Canada. She has Canadian and Danish citizenship. Her question was, what do you wish you still had?

She looked at the ceiling in contemplation and then said, "I wish I could still speak Chinese because that is the first language I was taught."

She was only a young child when she left China, yet she still had a desire to embrace her connection to China. It was still a part of her identity regardless of not being Chinese by citizenship or heritage. It is still a part of her story as it is where her life began, and she wants that

Chinese part of her to still be recognised. Because of my background on this topic, I think I was the only one in the circle who recognised how important what she said was. I doubt the others recognised this potion in her Cultural Cauldron as her physical attributes do not reflect someone who stereotypically should identify with China. In today's world physical attributes don't really mean or determine anything and that is a fact you need to take on board when telling your story.

When it got to my turn I pulled out a question and it asked, if you had to pick the perfect Saturday night, what would you be doing?

I also looked at the ceiling in contemplation then said, "I would be on the beach outside the Jumeriah Beach hotel in the evening, eating shawarmas and watching the sunset."

There were a couple oohs and aahs and my boss said, "Cool, very exotic."

To me my reply was not exotic, it felt homely. For me it is part of what I find comfort in because I have chosen to embrace the comfort that is experienced in Middle Eastern sunsets and I identify that I belong in that kind of environment. To me those moments in Dubai are the most peaceful times of the day when there are a few clouds in the sky and the sun sets into Iran making the windows of the Jumeriah Beach Hotel reflect back the golden light. It is a memory I have used during meditation to find that still, earthly peace. It is in this way that I continue to embrace the special attributes of Dubai that I carry within myself and feel that I am connected to. My identity to that homely comfort is a part of the potion of Dubai that is swirling around with the others in my Ultimate Potion.

Throughout the places I have travelled and lived in my life I have created a story influenced by the connections I have had with each place and the memories I have made there. I will never be fully from New Zealand; I will never be fully from America and I will never be fully from Dubai yet to me this is a great way to be. My story explains why I am not fully from one place, and it is a story that connects cultures and has a global experience. Personally, professionally, and societally this is a great way to be. When it comes to writing your story always know that the way you are, just the way you are with all your cultural blends, is a great way to be. My story is influenced by the comfort, identity and belonging I have found in places above and beyond citizenship, legality and technicality. Your mindfulness to your identity, belonging, definition of home and definition of the word from begins and stays sustainable when it is achieved first from within. It is in this way that you will create that strong diamond of who you are knowing that your perspectives are always welcome in this world despite what people think. Your perspectives are what the world needs to grow individual global mindsets. It all begins with you telling a part or all of your story of where you are from that is part of your identity.

Lorraine's Deep Dive of

YOUR STORY

AS THIS BOOK draws to a close, I recall the moment I shared at the beginning of what happened years ago when Ashley was a little girl. On the way home from school she had asked me to assist her with a school essay titled *Where Are You From.*

Her response back then baffled me. She had replied with a questioning tone, "This question *where are you from*, I do not actually know what it means."

The journey that Ashley and I have taken to dive into the nuances of this question have led us to seek to define our identity, our own personal story. The journey that Ashley and I have been on in writing this book has taken more than four years. It will be one of the highlights of my life. Conversations that spanned continents, hemispheres and countries as we connected first on Skype and then on Zoom. It has allowed me to reflect deeply on the journey one takes to come to terms with who they are and where they are from.

When Ashley and I spoke about how we would write this book we both knew that we wanted to share our week in Prague. The reason for this was to inspire you, the reader, to take time away from your busy schedules and daily to-do lists and find time to have conversations. Have conversations with people that you know in this situation and talk about the concepts in this book so that each of you can open up about difficulties you each have. By having conversations, it will also raise awareness for how other people's actions can affect someone who is not sure of who they are and is not fully confident in owning their identity and where they believe they are from. We chose to write this book in a way to share each of our thoughts, each from our own perspective, and each as our own deep dive. We did this because we wanted to give you a glimpse into each of our stories, connected as members of one family, but different. We chose to be vulnerable and to share stories in this book that we have never told others because we want our stories to inspire your stories.

We live in a world that is globally connected. We live in a world that has changed significantly in the past 20 years and continues to change and evolve. We live in a world that has been affected by a global crisis of the Covid pandemic. Who you are, where you are from, and how you define home can be challenging concepts to clarify today because our world continues to evolve and change. You do not have to have all the answers, you just need to remember that the answer to these questions is unique to you and will evolve as your life story evolves.

As you write and tell your story be sure to self-reflect and embrace your uniqueness, the special blend that makes you an original. Your story will contain elements similar to those found in other stories, yet it will maintain a celebration of the differences that make you a unique person. Research proves that people who make sense of their own life story, how it is all woven together and connected, have a greater sense of well-being. Your life's journey becomes your story made up of a collection of moments. It is your understanding of these moments and the meanings that you infuse into them that narrates your unique story.

My grandma use to say to me, "The wisdom we need to move forward is often found in reflecting on the past."

Just like Ashley and I have done throughout this book, you too will find greater wisdom in your story as you dive deep, reflect and seek to find understanding and clarity from all the parts of your past.

We are all storytellers, all engaged in an act of creation, the act of creating meaning out of our lives. Your description of your identity based on the experiences you have will continue to evolve. Narrating your own story based on your understanding is how you make sense of it all. By taking the disparate pieces of your life and placing them together into a narrative, you create a unified whole that allows you to understand who you are through the meaning that you attach to the experiences you have had. People who believe their lives are meaningful tend to tell their stories that reflect growth and positivity.

Today we live in a world where authenticity is key to developing both personal and professional relationships. Knowing who you are and how to communicate that through the messages and stories you tell is key to effective communication in a globally networked world today. Your identity is shared through a series of stories you tell yourself and others. Reframing your stories will provide a different perception of your identity, a better identity, a healthier outlook on the value you hold in your uniqueness. You are an integral part of our globally connected world today. You have understanding, wisdom and insights based on your unique blend. You are the catalyst through the conversations that you start and engage in that will collectively create a world of better understanding for all.

It is now time for you to write your story and that is the true finale to discovering how to answer the question *where are you from* because there is no set algorithm that can fit every Culturally Blended Person. You are the author of your own story as it continues to be written uninterrupted by the thoughts and perceptions of others. It is a story of your colourful cultural cauldron that adds beauty to our globally connected world.

ACKNOWLEDGMENTS

Ashley and I would like to acknowledge a group of people who have shared their personal experiences with us so that we could get a deeper understanding of the subject matter that was the inspiration for writing this book. Each person provided a different perspective of common themes allowing us to share their stories and experiences woven into ours. A very special thanks to Samir Malak, Kwong Yue Yang, Sepideh Moussavi, Suzanne Barrett, Saira Ranj, Konstantina Sakellariou, David Goecke, Rachel Boehm and Ankica Sweetman. We also listened to and read about the experiences of others who offered to share their stories. This input assisted us in having a greater understanding of the spectrum of unique details that are contained in individual stories of people that identify with being culturally blended. A special thanks to Zaahirah Muthy, Victoria Ferrer, Mathilde Fischer, Sally-Ann Davies, Lionela Toderian, and Karen Benn.

We would like to thank the members of the DO!brandYOU Community for their support and encouragement to move through the full process of writing and publishing.

Finally, we would like to share our sincere gratitude for the support and consistent encouragement that Wayne and Jennifer offered each step of the way.

CULTURALLY BLENDED PEOPLE COMMUNITY

Ashley and I have founded the Culturally Blended Community to be a safe place of support, friendship and belonging for people to continue the conversations that began in this book. Each person has their own story. As we share our stories, we listen and learn from each other.

I have been asked if the CBP Community is only for people that identify as a cultural blend. On the contrary, this community is fully open to anyone who wants to better understand this growing group of people that identify with being a cultural blend. These people include grandparents, parents, teachers, coaches, partners, community leaders and employers who are interested and invested in offering optimal ways to understand, assist and support a growing number of people that identify with being a cultural blend.

Learn more about the CBP Community and find out how you can become a member at:
culturallyblendedpeople.com

A FINAL MESSAGE FOR YOU

Thank you for taking the time to read *"Where Are You From?" A Question That Challenges Identity in a Culturally Blended World*. We hope that you enjoyed reading it as much as we enjoyed writing it.

Visit us at culturallyblendedpeople.com for updates and offers. We look forward to connecting with you personally.

If you found this book a valuable read, please take a moment to leave a review. This helps other people find this book.

- You can leave a review on the site that you bought the book, for example, Amazon.
- Or you can send a review to us personally using this link: bit.ly/review4whereareyoufrom
- Or visit the link using this QR Code:

We appreciate the time that you have taken to do this. Thank You.

Kind Regards,
Ashley and Lorraine

CPSIA information can be obtained
at www.ICGtesting.com
Printed in the USA
BVHW051936071022
648929BV00001B/157